Churn

ALSO BY
Claude M. Steele

*Whistling Vivaldi:
How Stereotypes Affect Us and What We Can Do*

Churn

THE TENSION THAT DIVIDES US AND HOW TO OVERCOME IT

CLAUDE M. STEELE

Liveright Publishing Corporation

*A Division of W. W. Norton & Company
Independent Publishers Since 1923*

Copyright © 2026 by Claude M. Steele

All rights reserved
Printed in the United States of America
First Edition

For information about permission to reproduce selections from this book, write to Permissions, Liveright Publishing Corporation, a division of W. W. Norton & Company, Inc., 500 Fifth Avenue, New York, NY 10110

For information about special discounts for bulk purchases, please contact W. W. Norton Special Sales at specialsales@wwnorton.com or 800-233-4830

Manufacturing by Lakeside Book Company
Book design by Marysarah Quinn
Production manager: Lauren Abbate

ISBN 978-1-324-09344-2

Liveright Publishing Corporation, 500 Fifth Avenue, New York, NY 10110
www.wwnorton.com

W. W. Norton & Company Ltd., 15 Carlisle Street, London W1D 3BS

Authorized EU representative: EAS, Mustamäe tee 50, 10621 Tallinn, Estonia

10 9 8 7 6 5 4 3 2 1

On behalf of the legacy they began, this book is for my parents, Ruth and Shelby Steele Sr.

CONTENTS

PROLOGUE XI

Introduction 1

CHAPTER 1: What Is Churn? 9

CHAPTER 2: Where Does Churn Come From? 27

CHAPTER 3: Churn Has an Antidote 39

CHAPTER 4: Being Wise, Not Color-Blind: How Individuals Can Build Trust Across Identity Divides 54

CHAPTER 5: Trust in the Face of Power 71

CHAPTER 6: Making School and Work Settings Wise 89

CHAPTER 7: Making Institutions Wise 105

CONTENTS

CHAPTER 8: **Making Guiding Paradigms Wise:**
K–12 Schooling and Low-Income Students. 131

CHAPTER 9: **Going Forward:**
A Perspective and a Strategy 154

CODA: **And Everyone Can Do It** 173

ACKNOWLEDGMENTS 181

REFERENCES 185

INDEX 191

Prologue

IMAGINE A REGULARLY SCHEDULED parent-teacher conference in an American middle school. The student in question is a seventh-grade boy. He and his parents are African American. His teacher is white. If you're an American, you may already sense a possible tension in the air. It's a meeting visited by American history, by the racial roles the parents and the teacher have been assigned by that history, and by the stereotypes that history has attached to those roles. For their part, the Black parents know how their group can be seen; they know this society's stereotypes about Blacks' intellectual potential and aggressiveness. They want desperately for their son not to be seen in these ways. They don't know that he is. But they know he could be. And schooling is so important. On the car ride over, they sort through their questions. Is this a good teacher? What's her style? Empathic? Tough love? Let's be sure not to jump the gun about race, they say to each other. But does she know anything about race? About bias? Does she push race under the rug—asserting color-blindness? Or is she comfortable with its realities? They enter the conference room vigilant, friendly but tense, poised to confront the ghosts of history if they have to. Their heads are in churn.

The white teacher has anxieties too as she prepares for this meeting. She knows the stereotypes about *her* group. She worries that saying anything that is less than totally positive about this student, even if it's intended to help his development, could get her seen as racist. She doesn't know that this will happen. But she knows it could happen. She would hate that. She tries to be fair to all her students—and sensitive to the needs of minority students. But how could these parents know that? She can't just claim she's not a racist. Entering the conference room, she too is vigilant, friendly but tense, worried about imagined and real trip wires. Her head, too, is in churn.

It's easy to imagine that this meeting might be a routine exchange—information given, resisted a bit, but largely received. Yet this meeting involves communicating between people of different identities—Black and white—identities that in this society have a history and a set of stereotypes attached to them. It's a "diverse" setting. And in such a setting, that history and those stereotypes can create ambiguity for both parties. How will their identities be perceived and responded to? Neither party knows for sure. They know the situation is too important to ignore, and that it could go badly. It's a question that haunts many exchanges in American society—between managers and employees, doctors and patients, lawyers and clients, police and the public, teachers and students, between colleagues, between friends. It's a question that arises from diversity itself. And it's a question that, in a diverse society like ours, makes churn a significant part of all our lives.

Churn

Introduction

SOMETIMES THE COMPLEXITY of a problem obscures a part of it that, if addressed, could greatly improve things. Take hospital-acquired infections, for example. These infections—pneumonia, bloodstream and wound infections, urinary tract infections—affect 1.7 million patients a year, killing as many as 99,000, according to the Centers for Disease Control and Prevention. They have complex causes—invasive procedures like surgery and catheterizations, immunocompromised patients, stethoscope contact, pathogens that resist antibiotics, and so on. Yet disciplined handwashing by hospital staff with antibacterial soaps and gels can reduce their occurrence by 50 to 70 percent. Handwashing isn't a cure-all. But it offers significant traction against these diseases.

Churn, too, is in search of traction against a complex problem: the tension that can exist between races, ethnicities, genders, social classes, generations, people of various sexual orientations, immigrant statuses, as we live and work together in the settings of our society—schools, workplaces, civic organizations, boardrooms, athletic teams, doctors' offices, courtrooms, and elsewhere. It's a tension that can undermine one's experience in these settings—one's ability to perform and to form relationships there, to feel safe from prejudice, to trust others. It can also affect how well a setting works—its productivity, trust in its governance and decision-making, the stability of its leadership, even its ability to meet the needs of different groups in the setting. *Churn* tries to do for this tension in American life what handwashing did for hospital-acquired diseases. It tries to identify an aspect of the problem that, if addressed, would help mitigate it—again, not as a cure-all, but as an underutilized road to progress. At base, *Churn* is a practical book. It focuses less on the nature or politics of identity and more on *what it takes to build trust* between people of different identities—even oppositional identities—in the real-life settings of our lives. It spotlights a dimension of human relations—trust-building—that may be even more powerful than we thought.

I COME TO THIS QUESTION from a background saturated in these concerns, in what I might call "America's expansion of opportunity project"—the effort to bring a society in which opportunity has been long stratified by identity (especially racial, ethnic, gender, and sexual orientation identities) into a society in which

INTRODUCTION

opportunity is less stratified, de jure or de facto, by identity. I was born to an interracial couple in Chicago on January 1, 1946, the day my sociologist friends tell me is the first day of the post–World War II baby boom. My father, African American, was born in 1900, and his father, my grandfather, was born in slavery in 1862. My mother, white, was born in 1915, the daughter of a construction company owner who built civic buildings in the small city of Ashland, Ohio. It's a family that has witnessed, from several vantage points and in many different eras, multiple ways in which racial and other identities have organized American society—from the end of slavery through Jim Crow and the civil rights movement, to the last sixty years or so of trying to use laws, public policy, and individual will to level the group playing field in our multi-racial, multi-ethnic society.

Looking at American life over this long period, I see a tug-of-war between forces pushing to broaden opportunity and those resisting it. To be sure, there have been major thrusts forward: *Brown v. Board of Education*, the 1954 Supreme Court decision desegregating American schools; the civil rights acts of the 1960s, which eliminated many of the laws that enabled the Jim Crow segregation we'd lived under until then; affirmative action policies that substantially expanded the middle class in minority communities by increasing their access to higher education and by pressing the institutions of government, academia, the military, and the corporate world to expand group access.

Yet fatigue with the pursuit of equality and inclusion has grown—a substantial tug in the opposite direction—and along with it, a political resistance to these efforts. Often rooted in zero-sum perceptions of minority gains, this resistance shape-shifts from anti-busing and anti–affirmative action movements to anti-DEI (diversity, equity, and inclusion) and anti–critical race theory movements. It has flown under different flags, but it has been, throughout American history, relentless.

At this point in the tug-of-war, resistance is in clear ascendance. The use of race-based affirmative action in college admissions was struck down in 2023 by the Supreme Court in *Students for Fair Admissions v. President and Fellows of Harvard College*. Busing as a means of racially integrating K–12 schools has been largely abandoned, even as our schools remain as segregated today as they were in 1954, when *Brown v. Board* outlawed school segregation. Presidential executive orders have opposed DEI programs in every walk of American life from education to the military. Many Americans, in this era, have wearied of the inclusion side of the tug-of-war. I have some sympathies. I am not blind to some of its excesses and limitations. For example, I am no fan of "cancel culture"—the opposite of the themes of this book. But I have long supported affirmative action as a form of reconciliation with our dominant racial, ethnic, and gender order, even while knowing that it can be used politically to fuel the resistive side of that tug-of-war. I am saddened by the tenor of the present moment. It's hard for me to imagine getting to the "post-racial," equal opportunity society we say we want without efforts of these sorts. We do have, after all, a debt to our past and the long shadow of identity-structured opportunity, disadvantage, status, and inequality that it casts over our present lives.

INTRODUCTION

While I am not giving up hope that we will find tools to address this responsibility, a question persists for me: How, in the midst of this resistance, can we get traction against the complexities that sustain this tug-of-war and the unfairness at its root?

Perhaps the chief idea has been to reduce prejudices that can unfairly fuel resistance—racism, sexism, anti-Semitism, classism, ableism, homophobia, xenophobia. Over and over, social science research shows the prevalence of human prejudice, both as conscious belief and as implicit, unconscious biases that can influence our behavior without our being fully aware of that influence. It's still easy to show that on average a classroom essay gets a better grade when it's attributed to a boy than when it's attributed to a girl, or to a white student rather than a Black student. It's easy to show that both Black and white police officers conducting a traffic stop tend to use more emotionally escalating language with Black drivers than with white drivers—behavior that the officers may or may not be aware of. It follows that an important route to fairness is to reduce these biases, to be identity-blind, to treat people as individuals, not as members of identity groups. And to be sure, this is a crucial standard of fairness. We want policing, access to health care, and access to neighborhoods and investment capital to be identity-blind, not meted out based on identity. And for prejudices that prove difficult to eliminate, we want to mitigate their unfair effects—as when musicians are auditioned from behind a screen so their sex won't influence judgments of their musicianship. Learning about the nature of prejudice, then, and how to reduce its effects, should be, I believe, part of everyone's education in any society.

Yet my role as a university administrator and my research on stereotype threat, described in my book *Whistling Vivaldi*, tell me that something else also makes integrating identities difficult. Something that affects the prejudiced and nonprejudiced alike. It's the threat, in the important settings of our lives, of being seen in terms of negative stereotypes about one of our identities. It's the threat felt in the parent-teacher conference described in the prologue. It's a threat inherent in diversity itself. Think of a setting in which a bad stereotype about one of your identities is relevant to what you're doing in the setting—as when a stereotype about aging and cognitive abilities is relevant to an older person taking a workshop on new technologies. If the setting is nondiverse—comprised of mostly older people—the older person can feel less at risk of ageist judgments. After all, his age mates are subject to the same judgments. They should be less inclined to make them against him—if not completely so, then substantially so. The absence of diversity in this setting gives him a "safe space." But if the setting is diverse—comprised of people of different ages—the older person could feel at greater risk of ageism.

This idea has become more compelling to me over the years. Put more generally: In settings that are important to us and where we could be devalued based on stereotypes about our identity, we feel safer with our own kind. We can surmise that our own kind won't be as likely to stereotype us. But as the setting includes more identities, this sense of safety can fade. And

INTRODUCTION

when the setting is important to us and our goals, this fading can be upsetting. It raises considerations that go beyond normal coping in the setting. Things like: How are people like me seen and treated here? Will I be supported here? Will it be a fair place for people like me? Diversity puts us in a state of mind in which identity is top of mind. Stressful emotions can arise. Thoughts scramble as we work to decipher and make meaning. To capture the anxious, ruminative nature of this state, my term for it is "churn," a term whose utility I suspect will increase as the diversity of our life settings increases.

This is because, with diversification, churn is an increasingly common experience for everyone—for teacher and parent alike in the parent-teacher conference, for example. And this raises important questions: Does the stress of churn lead people to avoid diverse settings? Does it make it difficult for people to flourish in them? If so, would practices that reduce churn—if we focused, for instance, on building trust between people of different identities—open new pathways to diversifying our institutions, schools, neighborhoods, civic organizations, even our personal relationships? Could they help depolarize our society? Could reducing churn—by making people more comfortable with each other—be a way of reducing prejudice itself?

I believe I've seen some of these things happen in my life and relationships, right from the beginning. But, just as important, considerable evidence can be brought to bear on these questions. So it is more than my intuition—though it is that too—that pushes me to take up these questions in *Churn*. Let's begin by taking a closer look at what churn is.

CHAPTER 1

What Is Churn?

|||||||||||||||||||||||

1.

Churn is the mental agitation and physical stress we can experience in diverse settings. Its immediate cause, as noted, is stereotype or identity threat—the threat of being judged and treated badly based on negative feelings or stereotypes about our identities: our religion, race, age, sex, sexual orientation. This threat begins with knowledge that virtually everyone has—of the feelings toward, and stereotypes about, the major identities in our society. Then, when we're in situations in which these feelings or stereotypes apply, this knowledge carries a threat: that we could be judged and treated in terms of those feelings and stereotypes. If the situation is important to us—that is, critical to things in our lives that we care about—we become worrisomely vigilant. Churn is precisely that worrisome vigilance.

Kazuo Ishiguro, the Japanese-born British novelist who won

the 2017 Nobel Prize in Literature, viewed his early books as "concerned [with] individuals who'd lived through times of great social and political upheaval, and who then looked back over their lives and struggled to come to terms with their darker, more shameful memories." He saw this as a tension between remembering and forgetting. Do his protagonists remember the past to truthfully understand themselves and their world? Or do they forget it to go forward unencumbered by a troubled legacy? Ishiguro sees this tension as a way of capturing how one's position in a society and its history shapes psychological experience. Churn, too, springs from a tension between remembering and forgetting. Does one **remember** how one's group can be disliked, negatively stereotyped, and treated in society? Does one then use that memory to interpret one's experience in an "integrated," diverse setting? Or does one **forget** those images and trust that somehow, in this particular setting, one won't be seen in those ways? This is the question that our use of *churn* is trying to answer. We don't know for sure that we will be put down by stereotypes in a situation. But we could be. And if the situation is important, we stay vigilant to that possibility and what to do about it. We remain in churn.

Stereotype threat is the threat, in situations important to us, of being judged and treated badly based on stereotypes about one of our identities. Churn is the psychological and physical reaction to that threat—the tension caused by vigilance to its possibilities. Churn, then, is a tension that can make coming together in diverse settings less appealing, less successful.

WHAT IS CHURN?

2.

Psychologists often use a simple task to measure how stressed people are. For each name of a color on a list, it asks people to name the color the name is printed in—as quickly as possible. When the name of the color—say, red—is printed in the same color as the word "red," people name the print color instantly. But when the name is printed in a different color—say, blue—they get momentarily confused. To answer correctly, they must inhibit the meaning of the word "red" and attend only to the color it's printed in—blue. This takes a bit more time. And when people are stressed about or vigilant to a threat in the setting, it takes even more time to resolve the confusion. In this way, the time it takes to say the print color of mismatched color names can measure how distracted by stress people are. This is called the Stroop test, after John Ridley Stroop, the person who invented it in the 1930s.

You can use the Stroop test, then, to ask if diversity is stressful. This is just what two brilliant social psychologists, Jennifer Richeson and Nicole Shelton, and their students asked in a program of research over several years—all built around the Stroop test. Their question was clear: Would a simple interaction between white and Black American strangers—a "diverse" interaction, if you will—be stressful enough to interfere with their performance on the Stroop test?

Their first experiment tested this question with white participants. Using college students, they staged either a *nondiverse interaction*—students answering questions about campus fraternities and racial profiling put to them by a white experimenter—or a *diverse interaction*, in which the same questions were put to them by a Black experimenter. As soon as these interactions were over (they lasted about five minutes), participants completed a Stroop test. That was it, the full experiment.

Later, a parallel experiment tested the same question with Black participants. In that experiment, college students had a conversation with either another Black student (a confederate of the experimenter) or a white student (also a confederate of the experimenter) about topics similar to the ones used in the experiment focused on whites. Then they too completed the Stroop test.

What happened? For white and Black students alike, the "diverse" interactions—those with other-race students—caused tension. They did worse on the subsequent Stroop test than when they interacted with same-race students. Even this modest level of diversity was enough to make members of both groups churn enough to impair their performance on the Stroop test.

Diversity, then, *can* be stressful under quite common circumstances. Not always. Foreshadowing a chief hope of this book, Richeson and Shelton show that, using classic measures of racial bias, people found to be less biased, and subjects who have had more intergroup contact, are less stressed by diversity. We should keep hope alive. Still, taken as a whole, the research makes one thing clear: "Diversifying" a setting can cause stress and churn unless something is done to mitigate the effect.

Virtually every identity is negatively stereotyped in some

way. When we are in situations that are important to us and where such stereotypes apply, we can worry about how having that identity will affect us. We churn. To see what this churn looks like in real life, let's expand the window.

3.

Here's a young white man who, in a Reddit post, gives words to what the white participants in the Richeson-Shelton experiments may have worried about:

> I have had this fear for a while now. I am white and am an advocate for all equality, especially the Black Lives Matter movement. I was called a racist a while back for asking why something was considered racist back when I was 13. And just recently I got called a racist for not holding the door for a person of color when I was on my way into work and did not look behind me. Now I find myself nervous to talk to my friends of color, whom I love dearly, not because of their color, but because I am scared of being called racist. I was wondering does this fear make me racist? I also have Autism which makes it hard for me to pick up on social cues, but that is no excuse. I apologize if I offend anyone with this question by the way. I will never know what it is like to be oppressed or experience microaggression because of my color. I'm not trying to be racist or ignorant by asking this question, I am just trying to learn.

This man is churning under the threat of being seen as racist—the stereotype about his identity that is relevant when he's with his friends of color, in a "diverse" situation. But of course churn happens to people of all groups, and certainly on both sides of a racial divide—as illustrated by the experience of a young African American woman on a hiking trail.

Mirna "the Mirnavator" Valerio is an outdoorswoman, a sponsored ultradistance trail runner (regularly competing in 50-mile races). She also loves biking, hiking, and almost any outdoor sport. But in the world of ultrarunners and long-distance hikers, there is something different about Mirna. In her words: "I'm a Black girl. A big girl." These sports and, tragically, outdoor recreational spaces more generally, have come to be seen in our society as more or less white spaces. Before Mirna became a well-known presence in these activities, she drew looks and comments when she'd show up at races or group hikes. People would say things like "you're kind of heavy to be out here running—maybe you should go to the gym." Other hikers would often check in with her to make sure she knew what she was is in for. She is better known now, thanks to several REI videos about her that went viral and her rise to the status of a sponsored athlete. Incursions on her sense of belonging are less frequent. Yet her remembering-versus-forgetting churn in these spaces persists. In her words:

> [Black people] are seen as nuisances in public spaces. There's research on that. I'm smiling because that's so heavy. To have to think about it constantly—and

WHAT IS CHURN?

> I do think about it constantly, every second that I'm on a trail. I mean, I may be smiling and I may be gracious, affable, but I am always, always thinking about whether or not people think I belong. Is somebody going to ask a dumbass question or are they going to say something stupid, or are they going to make me feel as though I'm not welcome? I'm always thinking of that. Which is why I'm so effusive with my cheer—because I have to be. . . . That's the story of every Black runner. Every single person who goes out and runs who is Black, we have to signal. . . . To signal to other people that we are safe to be around, and we are not a threat.

Both Mirna and the young man on Reddit are in churn over how their identities play out in situations that are important to them. And when churn is intense, it's not without consequences.

4.

Churn takes up bandwidth. It can be a tax in diverse settings. The churn of Mirna and our Reddit friend is emotion-laden mental work. Extra work. Work that neither of them would have to do if they weren't facing the identity threat that can come with diversity.

Research on this threat—"stereotype threat"—shows that churn like this can interfere with activities as far-ranging as athletics and standardized test-taking. The social psychologist

Joshua Aronson and I did one of the early experiments testing this. We invited white and Black Stanford University students into our laboratory one at a time and gave them a very difficult thirty-minute section of the verbal Graduate Record Examinations (GRE). These were strong students. We knew they'd see this test as important. But for Black students, we reasoned, there would be extra pressure. Any frustration they experienced (inevitable on such a challenging test) could make them worry about confirming or being seen to confirm the negative stereotype about their group's intellectual abilities that exists in American society. That is, it could make them churn, right in the middle of the test, about how their racial identity could shape how they were seen if they were in any way flustered on the test. And this churn in turn could get in the way of performance.

Two conditions of our experiment tested this idea: In one, we did nothing to reduce this pressure, and in the other we reduced the pressure by representing the test as not a test at all but rather as a lab "exercise" that had nothing to do with intellectual ability. This condition took away the threat to Black test-takers. Their frustration on it could not be seen as confirming the stereotype about their group's abilities, since it didn't measure these abilities. It was an "exercise," with no ability to diagnose intelligence.

What happened? Black students did significantly better when they believed the test could not measure their abilities than they did when they thought it could. When they thought it could, they churned. "Am I confirming the bad stereotype?"

WHAT IS CHURN?

"Might I be seen that way?" "What would this mean for my goals, for my life?" Churn diverts attention from the test. They did worse. But when they thought that the test was not about ability, they had no such worries. They could relax. With churn subsiding, they could focus on the test. They did better.

For white students, it didn't matter whether the test was presented as diagnostic or nondiagnostic of ability. They performed the same either way. There is no negative stereotype about their group's intellectual ability in this society. Thus there was no group stereotype that their frustration on the test could confirm. They were free of this pressure in both conditions.*

It's not that Black participants believed the stereotype

---

* Of course, white students can also underperform on standardized tests due to test-related anxieties—for example, a worry that parents or teachers would be disappointed by a poor performance, or that a poor performance would interfere with career goals, or that they lack a talent for standardized test-taking. Such anxieties can undermine anyone's test performance. The point here is that in addition to these pressures, Black students invested in academic achievement have an additional pressure—stereotype threat, the threat that they could confirm society's negative stereotype about their group's intellectual abilities. What this experiment shows is that when committed Black students experienced this risk (by virtue of taking a test diagnostic of intellectual ability), they did worse than when this risk was removed (by virtue of taking a test represented as nondiagnostic of ability). It shows that this risk, tied to their racial identity, is enough to impair their performance beyond whatever impairment might happen due to other anxieties.

White students' performance may have been impaired by anxieties too. But not by stereotype threat. There is no demeaning stereotype about their group's intellectual abilities in our society. So, unlike Black students in this experiment, they had no risk of confirming such a stereotype in either the diagnostic or nondiagnostic condition. Accordingly, they performed essentially the same in both conditions.

about their group. It's not that they had internalized it and then self-fulfilled it by giving up under the pressure of the test—as is perhaps the most common account of how group stereotypes affect us. Quite the contrary. These were strong students, probably hell-bent on disproving the stereotype. If anything, they were trying too hard. Being under the threat of a stereotype is different from self-fulfilling a stereotype. It's being in a predicament, a social-psychological predicament. It's having to contend with the real threat of being judged or treated in terms of a bad stereotype about your group. It's a threat in the air that derives from stereotypes rooted in our nation's history and the reaches of that history into the present. Right there in the middle of the test, these participants were contending with the far reach of American history and society. As William Faulkner famously said, "The past is never dead. It's not even past." The teacher in the parent-teacher conference, Mirna on the trail, the young man who made the Reddit post—all of them are dealing with a real threat in the air: the threat of how society will see and treat them based on images of their group . . . in areas of life they care about.

It's important to stress that it's not the stereotype alone, it's the *predicament* that matters—their wanting to do well on an inherently difficult test that, if they fail to do well on, could confirm a negative image of their group and of themselves as members of the group. That's the pinch. It's the combination of these elements that creates the disrupting pressure. As noted, these were strong college students who wanted to do well. If they hadn't wanted to, there would have been no pressure to perform, and therefore no predicament. The test was guaranteed to frustrate. If it didn't frustrate them, if they sailed through it, they'd never worry about confirming the stereotype. Again, no predicament. They were in a diverse environment where they knew the effect of the stereotype could be in play. If they were somewhere where the stereotype didn't exist or was weak—at a historically Black college or in, say, a Caribbean society—they'd have some assurance that they wouldn't be stereotyped in this way. Again, no predicament. So it's not the stereotype per se that impairs their performance. It's the stereotype plus who they are, what's important to them, the stiffness of the challenge they face, and whether they are in a setting that is diverse enough that the stereotype could be in play. It's these elements together that make a performance-impairing predicament.

Mirna's experience illustrates this. It's not the stereotypes about Black or large people alone that trouble her. She would, of course, despise these stereotypes. But it's all the elements of her situation—her wanting so badly to do difficult athletic feats in environments where she knew she could be painfully stereotyped—that comprise her predicament.

There is poignancy to stereotype threat: It's felt most by those in the stereotyped group who are most identified with achieving in the area where the stereotype applies, and who are trying to do challenging or frustrating things in that area. It affects most the vanguard of the group—as in Mirna wanting to succeed as an ultrarunner; as in women trying to break glass ceilings in finance; as in highly invested African American law students taking challenging state bar exams; as in white American males trying to succeed in elite basketball. That's when, in the heat of frustration, the stereotype's dark message—"everybody knows that, because of who you are, you probably can't do that well at this, and that you probably don't belong"—becomes personally relevant. That's when it can cause enough churn to interfere with performance.

Science not only seeks significant findings but also assesses their strength and importance—that is, subjects them to further tests of their replicability and generalizability, as well as exploring their important implications. The phenomenon of stereotype threat has enjoyed a truly exceptional amount of this kind of scientific attention. In the last thirty years, hundreds of experiments and field studies have tested and explored stereotype threat and the factors that affect its strength—involving different groups, different stereotypes, and different kinds of performance and behavior, both inside the laboratory and in real-life settings. Many meta-analyses and replications of this research have shown stereotype threat effects on memory performance in older adults, on negotiating behavior in women, on performance among elite athletes, on physiological indicators of stress, and on standardized test performance among African Americans and women. And when elements of the stereotype threat predicament are present and strong, these effects can be substantial.

But what exactly happens when we churn? What is happening to Mirna's thinking and emotions as she integrates into a group of endurance hikers?

5.

Summarizing their own and others' research, a distinguished group of Canadian psychologists led by Toni Schmader (Schmader, Michael Johns, and Chad Forbes) points to three things that typically happen when people are under this threat. First, they're stressed. Their heart rate, blood pressure, and sweating are elevated. Activity in their prefrontal cortex is often suppressed—which makes it more difficult to control attention, thinking, emotions, and behavior. It's harder to engage in the task at hand. Second, they're self-conscious. They exhort themselves to double down, to disprove the stereotype. Then they monitor themselves to see if their efforts are working. Third, they try to suppress negative thoughts that, if allowed to surface, would deepen their sense of threat.

This is what can happen when we're in diverse settings that are important to us. It's what happened to Mirna on the hiking trail, to the white teacher and Black parents in the parent-teacher conference, to the African American students during the frustrating parts of the standardized test. They were aroused. They continually monitored themselves to see if they were confirming the stereotype. They searched for clues to the severity of the threat. They remembered yet tried to forget. They were distracted, less focused, socially awkward. Such churn becomes exhausting, especially if it's in their lives for a prolonged amount of time. As it is for people pursuing a career or avocation in settings where they are working against stereotype-driven low expectations, as in Mirna's experience on hiking trails or in the experience of an Asian American basketball player in the National Basketball Association.

An understandable response to this is: "Why don't people in these predicaments just buckle down, ignore the stereotype, and do their best to disprove it?" Importantly, that is precisely what most people in this predicament are trying to do. And sometimes it works. When the task is relatively easy, research shows that the stereotype threat predicament—and the extra motivation to disprove the stereotype it causes—can actually improve performance.

But it's a different story when the task is difficult enough to cause frustration—when it's at the frontier of one's skills, so to speak. The experience of frustration gives credence to the stereotype. It tells the person: "Given your frustration, maybe the stereotype is true, and true of you," or "Given your frustration, maybe others will see the stereotype as true, and true of you." For people who care about doing well on the task, both ideas are upsetting, threatening. They try to forget—they try to forget the stereotype and push on. But the frustration makes them remember. It makes them confront the stereotype—the possibilities it raises. They have to deal with it—sometimes consciously and sometimes unconsciously—as a distracting tension. This pushes them into a churn of self-exhortation to do their best, and self-monitoring to see if their efforts are working. This churn happens, of course, as they're trying to do the task at hand. They're essentially multitasking. Compared to somebody not in this predicament, they have less attention and energy for the task, be it a standardized test, as in the above experiment,

WHAT IS CHURN?

or a parent-teacher conference, where all involved are affected. A fact that can impair functioning in both situations.

6.

But is stereotype threat different from the threat caused by any possible negative judgment? For example, knowing that your Aunt Joyce thinks you like to show off your cooking, you might be anxious about her judgment as you prepare the sweet potato dish for her Thanksgiving dinner. You might churn: Should you add the key lime sauce or not?

What's different about stereotype threat? First, group stereotypes are often meaner than personal judgments of other people—alleging, for example, a lack of intelligence, full humanity, or a capacity for human decency. Interpersonal judgments aren't generally so dehumanizing. But more important, interpersonal judgments come from one person—Aunt Joyce, in this case—or from a small group of people. Your vulnerability is limited to the reaches of that one person or group. But everybody knows the stereotypes and the status structures that prevail in a region—your family knows, your teachers know, your friends know, your work colleagues know, strangers know, they all know the stereotype allegations against your identity. Anytime you're in a situation where those allegations could apply, there is threat: You know you could be seen and treated in terms of those allegations. And you know that *this judgment or treatment could come from anybody in the setting.*

Mirna knows that she could be stereotyped by anyone on the trail, anytime. This is a lot worse than knowing, for example, that one hiker doesn't like her or several hikers don't like her. She knows that *all* of them know the stereotypes about her identities. And even if a few people on the trail don't seem to stereotype her, she knows others could. She stays vigilant. She keeps remembering. Identity threat, in this way, is more blanketing than the threat of interpersonal judgments. It's there anywhere the stereotype applies, and in those settings, it can come from anybody, anytime.

Imagine this playing out in important settings like school, the workplace, or public spaces. Being haunted by a dehumanizing stereotype about your group's humanity, intelligence, or goodness can keep one in remembering mode, as a painful condition of life.

Think of the Asian grandmother living in the center of a major city, getting out her cloth grocery bags for a trip to the neighborhood farmers market. Images flash across her mind of women who look like her being pushed to the ground and kicked and of their assailants scurrying off. She may know something of the eleven thousand hate crimes in the United States over the past year. Can she assume that she won't be next? Perhaps. But at another level she knows that out there on the streets she has a threat tied to her identity as an Asian woman: She, too, for no reason, and despite being small and in her eighties, could be pushed to the ground. In the US at this point, the simple anticipation of being in a public space can put her in churn.

Is it any surprise that people might want to leave such settings—be it a classroom, a diversity training workshop, a hiking trail, or an urban farmers market? Mirna is clearly courageous. She hikes despite her unceasing discomfort on the trail. But she's probably an exception to the rule. Most of us weary of churn. We look for refuge—settings where the stereotype doesn't apply, or where the people in the setting share the identity in question so we can feel less vulnerable. Few Blacks seem to have joined Mirna on the hiking trail. Identity threat can be life-shaping, pushing people in and out of settings, even in and out of whole walks of life.

So it's a lot worse than the threat of Aunt Joyce's judgments or for that matter most other judgments you might encounter. In important settings where the stereotype applies, it can blight one's life.

7.

Importantly, the stereotype threat framework can give us a line of sight into other groups' experiences of identity. An empathic line of sight. Their identity threat is essentially a version of our identity threat. It could be a greater or lesser version. That would depend on the conditions that produce the threat, and how chronic those conditions are in our lives. Think of damning group stereotypes that apply to many important settings—stereotypes, for example, that allege your group's cruelty or lack of intelligence. The threat of such a stereotype can blanket your life—putting you under a dark suspicion in many settings, including the most important in your life, such as school and the workplace. Stereotypes about race, ethnicity, and sexual orientation often have this character. Whereas being vulnerable to a less damning group stereotype that applies in less important settings—for example, that your group lacks fashion sense or that you are bad dancers—would be less threatening and less blanketing of your life, more of a passing experience.

Still, if you feel the heat of this threat in one situation—you're a white male participating in an intense diversity training—that experience might give you insight into what a woman feels like as one of a small minority in an advanced STEM seminar. The groups are different. The situations are different. The relevant stereotypes are different. But the predicaments are analogous. They have the same form: being under the threat of a bad group reputation in a situation one cares about. Recognizing this analogy, then, can be the seed of intergroup empathy.

This book is not about how we perform under the weight of this predicament. It's about our ability to get along with each other under its weight, across identity divides, in diverse settings. It's about how to reduce churn, lighten its load, and enable us to form community despite the divides that our history and culture have left us. The civil rights era launched our national commitment to a fully integrated society. Integration 1.0. This book, benefiting from the sixty or so years since that commitment, asks how we can make it work better. It's in search of Integration 2.0.

But first, what exactly is it that pushes us into churn in the face of difference?

CHAPTER 2

Where Does Churn Come From?

1.

Two events in my youth introduced the word "prejudice" into my active vocabulary. I learned of the first event when, as a nine-year-old, I boarded a bus at 119th and Halsted in Chicago and found, on the seat next to me, a copy of *Jet*—a weekly magazine that was broadly distributed in African American communities—that someone had left behind. Inside was a picture of the mutilated head of Emmett Till lying in his casket. Till was the fourteen-year-old African American boy who had been murdered on August 28, 1955, in Money, Mississippi, by two white Mississippians for allegedly whistling at Carolyn Bryant, a twenty-one-year-old white woman who decades later confessed that critical details of her account of the flirtation had never happened. Till's mother wanted the casket open so that the world could see the terror African Americans lived under in

Mississippi. I, along with virtually everyone who saw that picture, was deeply unsettled by it.

The other event was a CBS or NBC television newsreel broadcast, in the early 1950s, of film footage from the US military or the Nuremberg trials showing massive Nazi rallies and the horror American troops saw as they entered the death camps at the close of World War II. These were the George Floyd moments of that era—publicly broadcast cruelties that revealed humans' unfathomable capacity for hatred and violence toward people *based on their identity*. "Prejudice," I kept hearing, was the source of such evil.

I remember my mother being undone by these events. In addition to her own alarm, she seemed confused about how to talk to us, her children. She hemmed and hawed. She seemed to want us to understand these events. But she seemed to worry: Was it wise to let children see this darkest side of the human character? Was it wise to give them the knowledge that people could do these things to others—including them—based on who they were, on their identity alone? I overheard her talking to friends about this. In the end, she was a down-to-earth Midwesterner. She took things head-on. So, she talked and talked. The word "prejudice" anchored what she said. Her talking helped. Things weren't so bad that they couldn't be talked about. But a certain innocence was lost. I had a new lens through which to see people: they could be "prejudiced" toward you based on who you are. And that could be dangerous. You had to pay attention—an introduction, perhaps, to what I am now calling "churn."

WHERE DOES CHURN COME FROM?

Soon, in the larger society, a broader perspective emerged: Evils like these could come from people who were not especially warped in some way. In fact, they could come from the escalation of ordinary human tendencies—tendencies like obedience to authority, conformity to in-group norms, and ambition to succeed in the bureaucratic regimes in which we live and work. These tendencies could blind or desensitize us to the consequences of our actions, even when those consequences were as horrific as what occurred in Nazi Germany. Hannah Arendt famously called this "the banality of evil."

I'm not sure that "the banality of evil" is a full account of the horrors I mention here. Some derangement—individual or collective—would also seem necessary. Still, it's possible that some *ordinary* tendency of the human psyche might be involved, some tendency that makes us especially vigilant to group identity.

A famous experiment suggests precisely this. And it is perhaps no accident that it comes from the research program of Henri Tajfel, a social psychologist who himself was a Jewish prisoner of war during World War II.

Tajfel famously asked fourteen- and fifteen-year-old boys to judge the number of dots in clusters of dots that he flashed on a screen in front of them. Then he told each boy, *on a completely random basis*, that he was either an "over-dot-estimator" or an "under-dot-estimator." That is, he put the boys in groups that differed in an essentially meaningless way. You'd expect, then, that their group assignment would have no effect on how they treated each other. But it did. When he later asked the boys to rate each other's character and allocate rewards among them, he found that they favored their own estimator group—"unders" favoring "unders," and "overs" favoring "overs." They had no history with these identities, no idea of what they could mean. Other research by Tajfel and his colleagues examined this effect under different conditions, such as when participants divided money between the groups. But one thing remained clear: The mere fact of their segregation into groups, arbitrary as it was, made them defenders of their new identities.

A feature can be meaningless in its own right—like dot-estimation tendencies or skin color. But once it's used to divide people into groups, it becomes significant to us. We want to know why. What is it about dot estimation or skin color that makes this division necessary? We build explanatory narratives. We churn. And we prefer narratives that put our group, and thus ourselves, in a good light ... and perhaps other groups in a lesser light. We build an understanding of the divide that flatters us and our group. As an under-estimator, for example, I might begin to think that we under-estimators have special strengths—goodness, cleanliness, intelligence—and that over-estimators, bless their hearts, simply have less of these things. It doesn't take much of an identity divide, even a self-evidently meaningless one, to mobilize a self-enhancing churn that gives the divide a feeling of being natural, even preordained.

And before you know it, these narratives become broadly known. They become stereotypes. Even when the feature on which they are based is meaningless. And stereotypes have a power of their own. They survive past the segregations that spawned them. They bring the past into the present. They follow members of the stereotyped groups into situations where they could apply. They threaten them there with the possibility of being judged and treated in terms of them. They're the ghosts of history that the parents and teacher in the opening story of the book were contending with.

This process, then, can elevate a group division—even if meaningless—into a dimension along which a society is organized and stratified, a dimension along which things like status and opportunity are allocated. Over-estimators, for example, becoming higher-status than under-estimators. We wouldn't really know why—except for the stereotypes we develop to explain it to ourselves. But soon the division becomes part of the social order of a society, a social order so well explained by stereotype narratives that we experience it as the natural order of things, a received order.

In her book *Caste*, Isabel Wilkerson uses the brilliant metaphor of a stage play to illustrate how a skin color hierarchy is sustained in modern society even though it evolved not rationally but through a system of historical oppressions and incidental follow-on effects.

> Day after day, the curtain rises on a stage of epic proportions.... The actors wear the costumes of their predecessors....
>
> The costumes [racial identity and skin color] were

handed out at birth and can never be removed. The costumes cue everyone in the cast to the roles each character is to play....

For generations, everyone has known who is center stage.... who the hero is... who is the sidekick good for laughs, and who is in shadow, the undifferentiated chorus with no lines to speak, no voice to sing, but necessary for the production to work....

[E]veryone begins to believe... that each cast member is best suited by talent and temperament for their assigned role.

THE KINDS OF IDENTITIES at the center of *Churn* are not passing identities, like being an over- or under-estimator of dots. They are identities that have come down to us through this long process of identity stratification. They are identities that have significance in the American social order. They reflect our use of features like race, ethnicity, indigeneity, and sexual orientation to stratify and organize society—to develop and assign roles in Wilkerson's American stage play. Since Europeans landed in the Americas, we've used identity to do this, to decide who would be fully in the American social contract, who would be outside that contract in the sense that they could be enslaved or have their lands appropriated, and who would be disadvantaged in the ongoing allocation of resources and opportunity in society. And we've developed a bundle of stereotypes to justify those role assignments. This long tradition of identity politics has made us a society substantially organized by identity. For most of our history, for example, Blacks, Latinos, Asians, and Native Americans have had lesser roles in Wilkerson's stage play than Americans of European descent. They were pressed into "segregated" communities, which were maintained by law, discriminatory practices, neglect, and terrorism. Gays, too, have been traditionally excluded from social acceptability.

But in the 1950s and 1960s, the civil rights movement ushered in a series of legal decisions: *Brown v. Board of Education*, desegregating American schools; the 1964 Civil Rights Act, outlawing discrimination in public facilities; the 1965 Voting Rights Act, prohibiting racial discrimination in voting; the Fair Housing Act of 1968, which prohibits discrimination by landlords, real estate companies, municipalities, banks, and homeowners insurance companies; and the Immigration and Nationality Act of 1965, outlawing de facto discrimination against immigrants from southern Europe, Asia, and elsewhere. These decisions committed the United States to a new social order, one that would jettison the identity segregations of the past and build an "integrated" society in which people would not be discriminated against based on identity. We still struggle in the twenty-first century, perhaps even more so in recent years, to fulfill these commitments. And the old order casts a long shadow over contemporary American life. As noted earlier, our schools are as racially segregated today as they were before school segregation was outlawed by the Supreme Court in 1954.

Still, we made a commitment. Instantiated it in law. Gave it moral traction. We may be the only society in the world to do so, at least so explicitly. It's an experiment. Perhaps *the* American experiment. And we've been running it now for seventy-plus years. At the core of that experiment is a challenge we haven't well understood. A challenge unmet—a fact that drags on that commitment like an anchor to the past.

2.

Diversity is the bringing together, in a single setting—a school, civic meeting hall, neighborhood, workplace, church, classroom—of people whose identities offer a range of different experiences. People whose identities have occupied different roles in Wilkerson's play. It wouldn't be too much to say that it is the bringing together of people who, considering our nation's history, may not easily trust each other—white and Black, Christian and Muslim, LBGTQ and straight, high- and low-income, more and less educated. The parents and teacher in the opening vignette illustrate the possibility of mistrust in such diverse settings—perhaps the central predicament of the American experiment.

When we move out of identity-segregated communities into diverse communities—entering college, the military, many parts of the corporate world, or joining an athletic team—there's often a price to pay. It increases our chances of being seen and treated as a stereotype—through the lens of negative stereotypes of our group that exist in the larger society. When we're with only our identity mates, we can feel relatively free of this threat. We share with them the same identity. And we're outside the gaze of the larger society. As an African American, I like Black barbershops for this reason. Others like their own affinity groups. Women their women's groups. Still others, their identity-homogeneous country clubs. There's security in in-group spaces. But when we move into diverse settings, that security weakens. We're now with people who *could* see us more invidiously, in terms of negative stereotypes and images of our group. We don't know that they will. But we know they could. We know they know the stereotypes. And we know they could see us accordingly. So if the situation is important to us, we become vigilant, on edge.

This, I would suggest, is the social tension at the heart of the American experiment. It's what makes us churn. In diverse settings we have questions: "Given my identity and the stereotypes about it, can I trust this situation?" "Will I be valued here?" "Treated fairly?" "Will I be heard here?" The struggle to answer these questions—to figure out how one's identity will play out in a situation—is what churn is.

3.

Importantly, though, it's not a burden borne equally by all groups.

If your group is traditionally confined to lesser roles in the Wilkerson play, it's harder to escape churn-inducing pressures. Think of the difference between the white schoolteacher and the African American parents. Both parties are stressed by the parent-teacher conference itself. They're both dealing with stereotype threats tied to their identity. But outside of that conference, in the rest of their lives, the status and power associated with their group identities makes a difference. There, the white schoolteacher likely has an advantage. Due to our society's lingering history of racial and class segregation and inequality, it's possible for many white Americans to live in predominantly white communities—in their schools, churches, workplaces, neighborhoods, civic organizations, retirement homes, friendship networks. These communities shield one from the pressures of diversity. In them, people can meet most of their needs without much contact with equal-status people of different group identities, people who could see them stereotypically. The white schoolteacher, for example, might have little experience with diversity outside of the parent-teacher conference itself. In her world, people are for the most part just individuals. The idea of group identity can seem foreign. It's only through her infrequent encounters with diversity—and the identity threat it can pose—that she gets a sense of even having a "racial identity." It's diversity that racializes her.

The African American parents face a different world outside of the parent-teacher conference. They, too, are racialized by diversity. But for them it is a more common experience. To work, be educated, get health care, buy food and clothes, they must regularly transact with people of different identities—often of greater social power and status—who may see and treat them stereotypically. Their day involves more diversity than does the teacher's day. And that diversity can blanket their lives with the threat of stereotype-based devaluation, keeping them in churn much of the time.

WHERE DOES CHURN COME FROM?

In her book *The Trayvon Generation*, Elizabeth Alexander, the renowned African American poet and president of the Mellon Foundation, wonders if this burden doesn't sometimes cause a "low-grade, undiagnosed depression," especially in the young. She detects it "in the vision of television shows like *Atlanta* and *Insecure*" written by young African Americans. She believes it reflects the "specter of race-based violence and death that hangs over these young people"—something the media makes it difficult to escape. She sees it further "compounded" by the "constant display of inequity... laid bare in the COVID-19 pandemic, with racial health disparities that are shocking even to those of us inured to our disproportionate suffering." The surges of violence against Asian Americans, Jewish Americans, Arab Americans, and LGBTQ Americans place them in a similar predicament—having to live important parts of their lives in transaction with a potentially menacing mainstream society. Recall the Asian grandmother gathering her shopping sacks for a trip to the neighborhood farmers market.

4.

Despite the Declaration of Independence's assertion that "all men are created equal," the commitment to a diverse society in which all Americans have equal status in the social contract is relatively new, post–civil rights. Yet so many of our institutions were established in the decades and centuries before that commitment, and likewise so much of the organization of our society and so much of its culture, pedagogies, operating systems, systems of opportunity. Thus many of society's institutions and systems weren't designed to serve the full diversity of the population.

Through much of the post-civil rights era, we've tried to address this. We've tried to build the societal and institutional capacities needed to fulfill this commitment to all citizens—through federal legislation (from the Civil Rights Acts to affirmative action policy and diversity, equity, and inclusion institutional programing), a vast number of local political and legal actions, broad cultural change (witness the increasing diversity of television commercials), and so on. The resistance to these efforts notwithstanding, I have long felt that we—as a society in the making—deserve some credit for the spirit of reckoning they represent.

Yet as noted in the introduction, at this point in the American tug-of-war between inclusion and resistance, resistance is in ascendance—putting many of this era's achievements at risk and restricting the tools that can be used to address the challenges of diversity. We face the following question: What is the path forward? Is there something that, in the diverse settings of our lives, can help meet these challenges, that can reliably lower the tension, the churn between us?

CHAPTER 3

Churn Has an Antidote

1.

A Bronx Tale is a movie about a young man named Calogero who in the mid-1960s comes of age in an Italian neighborhood in the Bronx, a part of New York City that sat cheek by jowl with an African American community—two rival communities wasting no love on each other. Calogero's life is caught between two mentors: his father, who is a bus driver, and a local mob boss named Sonny. At age nine, Calogero witnessed Sonny kill a man, yet he didn't snitch to the police. Sonny owes Calogero and in time comes to love him as a son. In his late teens, Calogero develops a crush on a beautiful African American girl from his high school named Jane Williams. But given the deep animosities between their communities, he is in churn. Could she ever get past those animosities? Could she ever like him? Won't she see him as the African American community sees all Italian boys—as hoodlums to be avoided at all costs?

Surprisingly, Sonny empathizes with Calogero. He gives him a way of testing Jane's feelings for him: the "door" test. As Calogero gets out of his car to pick Jane up for a movie, he is to lock all the doors. When he later escorts her to the front passenger door, he is to unlock it and make sure she's comfortably seated. Then, as he walks around the rear of the car to get to the driver's side, he is to notice whether Jane leans over to pull up the lock button on the driver's door. (Remember, early-sixties cars had manual lock buttons on each door that, if lifted, could unlock the door from the inside.) If she does this, Sonny says she's capable of thinking of others. She's trustworthy. A marriage prospect. But if she doesn't, if she forces him to use his key to unlock the driver's door, Sonny says she's too self-centered to be a good marriage prospect. "All you're seeing is the tip of the iceberg," he says. A tough test indeed. But then the moment arrives. Calogero gallantly escorts Jane to the passenger seat. And as he walks around the rear of the car to get to the driver's side, he sees Jane, in one graceful motion, lean over to unlock the driver's door for him. He jumps for joy. He can trust her feelings. He can trust Jane. His churn gives way to conviction.

2.

In a single gesture, Jane deepens Calogero's trust. A question arises: How does that gesture affect Calogero's thinking about Jane going forward? Is there a way he thinks about Jane *after* she unlocked the car door that is different from the way he thought about Jane *before* she unlocked the car door? And the deeper question: Do we think differently when we trust than when we mistrust?

A team of social psychologists led by the Israeli psychologist Yaacov Schul offered a theory. When we mistrust, they argue, we resist the dominant understanding of a situation. We counterargue. This prepares us for the possibility that the dominant understanding is wrong. Jane tells Calogero, "I like Italians"—an understanding that both parties would like to dominate their early relationship. But the animosity between their communities makes Calogero mistrust her. He resists her words. He tells himself she probably doesn't like him. He prepares for the worst. He doesn't drop his preferred understanding—that she could like him. He keeps both ideas in mind: She loves me, she loves me not. He churns.

But with trust, the Schul team argues, we allow ourselves to believe. We go with the dominant understanding of a situation. After Jane unlocked the car door, Calogero no longer doubted her; he no longer hectored himself with opposing understandings. He allowed himself to believe, simply: "She loves me." Churn subsided.

The Schul team designed an experiment to test this view of trustful and mistrustful thinking. They first put participants in either a trusting or mistrusting mindset (by showing them human faces that were either trusting—with rounded, open eyes—or mistrusting—with narrowed, squinting eyes). Then, for word pairs that had either a clear dominant meaning (for example, "transient" and "temporary") or no dominant meaning ("permanent" and "temporary"), they measured how fast the participants could answer the question "Is the second word of the pair a noun or a verb?"

They reasoned as follows: If trust makes people more willing to accept dominant meanings in a situation, then participants who have been put in a trusting mindset should quickly accept a dominant meaning if it exists (as in the word pair "transient" and "temporary") and move on to answer the question about whether the second word in the pair is a noun or a verb. But if the word pair has no dominant meaning ("permanent" and "temporary"), they might struggle a bit looking for such a meaning and take longer to get to the question.

The opposite should hold for people in a mistrusting mindset. They're skeptics. They're set to resist the dominant meaning of a word pair. Their resistance should be strong when the word pair has a dominant meaning ("transient"/"temporary")—stronger than when it has no dominant meaning ("permanent"/"temporary"). That is, it should take them *longer* to move on to the question when the word pair has a dominant meaning than when it has no dominant meaning.

This is just what happened. Trusters (participants shown faces with rounded, open eyes) answered the question faster when the word pairs had a dominant meaning, and mistrusters (people shown faces with narrowed eyes) answered it faster when the word pairs had no dominant meaning.

When we trust, we accept. When we distrust, we resist. We look for alternative meanings and scenarios. And if the situation is important, we do this a lot; we churn.

CHURN HAS AN ANTIDOTE

This close-up picture of trustful and mistrustful thinking clarifies something: What brings on trustful thinking and the cessation of churn is some signal that a person or situation is indeed trustworthy. This could be an open face with round eyes, a potential paramour unlocking the car door for us, inclusive features in a classroom. *These signals evoke trust. They calm churn.* They're churn's kryptonite.

Hence a question: Could such signals have reduced the churn of the Black parents and the white teacher in their parent-teacher conference described in the prologue—the teacher, for example, having reached out earlier to the parents for advice about, say, a reading assignment or a field trip before the conference about their son, or the parents having volunteered to help chaperone a field trip? Could such signals generally foster acceptance between people on edge with each other because of identity threat? Could they improve the functioning of diverse institutions and organizations? Could they unlock a better America?

3.

The common presumption is that biases like racism, sexism, and homophobia are the chief corrosives of diversity. And they *are* bad, to be sure. What I'm arguing is that churn is a further corrosive—in many common situations, as corrosive as prejudices themselves. Is the white teacher avoiding a needed conversation with Black parents because she is prejudiced, or because she is worried that a misstep in the conversation could get her seen as racist? Is it prejudice? Or is it churn that makes her hesitate? The point is that reducing churn can sometimes be as important in diverse settings as reducing prejudice itself.

Admittedly, this idea asks for an expansion of our thinking. Assuming that group prejudices—as in the hatred between the Black and Italian communities in *A Bronx Tale*—are the chief barriers to an identity-integrated society, we've developed a strategy for achieving that society: color-blindness or, more broadly, identity-blindness. The reasoning is straightforward. If prejudices like racism, sexism, and homophobia are the barriers to an integrated society, then shouldn't we try to see past identity, the very thing on which these "isms" are based? Shouldn't we see and treat people as individuals? Isn't that our moral responsibility as people committed to an integrated society? I'm old enough to remember the emergence of this idea as a progressive idea in the 1960s. It offered a strategy by which we might overcome our segregated past.

And, as noted, color- or identity-blindness *is* an incontestable standard of fairness in many parts of society. As noted earlier, we want our policing, our access to health care, and our access to home mortgage financing to be color-blind.

Yet limitations of this approach have emerged. First, we know now that it's difficult to actually be color-blind. Research on unconscious bias, for example, shows that bias is often rooted in simple associations between group identities and reputed tendencies—associations picked up from the world around us without much awareness (for example, women—home; men—work; Blacks—aggressive, and so on). These associations in turn can shape our judgments and actions without our being consciously aware of it. As noted in the introduction, it's still possible to show that the same essay may get graded higher when its author is presumed to be male than when its author is presumed to be female—a bias shown by women as well as men and which exists largely beneath conscious awareness. This doesn't mean we just have to live with the bad effects of bias. But it does mean that trying to mitigate its effects can be as important as trying to eliminate it altogether.*

Second, the effort to be identity-blind can actually cause a certain blindness: not seeing the conditions of life that people deal with because they have an identity—*identity contingencies*, as I have called them. Most readers are familiar with the tragic end of George Floyd's life at the hands of Derek Chauvin, a Minneapolis police officer, on May 25, 2020. But we're less familiar with the conditions under which George Floyd grew up, conditions he contended with not because he was George Floyd the individual but because he was George Floyd, an African

---

* We are learning more about how to mitigate the effects of bias. In the introduction, I mentioned the practice of having musicians audition for orchestras from behind screens so that their sex and race won't affect listeners' judgment of their playing. Research by Jennifer Eberhardt and her students suggests that requiring police officers to use protocols that slow down and deescalate traffic stops (requiring them to record the purpose of the stop before approaching the driver, or that give them deescalating scripts to guide officer-driver interactions) can reduce the influence of bias, unconscious or conscious. In some walks of life, we've long understood the importance of bias mitigation. Think of our separation of church and state, or the body of conflict-of-interest law and regulations. Bias can be thought of as a virus, something difficult to eliminate entirely but whose bad effects can sometimes be mitigated.

American born and raised in a low-income African American community. These are communities with unemployment rates often three times the national average. The wealth per capita is less than a tenth of that for white Americans.

Jobs that do exist in these communities are often unstable and involve extreme and irregular working hours. Such was the case for George's mother, Missy, a single mother. Older children in these communities often supervise, cook for, and manage the activities of younger children—this was George's role in his household. There would be little time available to prepare a young George for school.

His relatively isolated community lacked a lot of the cultural capital he needed to thrive in our educational systems, places where he might have found a pathway to greater social and economic security. Instead, immediate family needs dominated his existence, and the family lacked the resources to help him navigate his schooling. When he did get to school, it was an institution dramatically under-resourced, with the least well-trained teachers, with harsh disciplinary practices, and located in a neighborhood troubled by gangs and drugs.

As a large, well-coordinated African American boy, the encouragement he got from teachers focused on his athletic talents. No one encouraged him academically. He remembered one of his teachers saying: "Hey, you football players. If you guys just be quiet and sit in the back, I'll pass you." If he got in trouble outside of school, he faced a biased criminal justice system, as the tragic end of his life illustrated. Throughout his

CHURN HAS AN ANTIDOTE

life he had limited access to quality health care and even to quality food.

He faced these conditions not because he was George Floyd the individual but because of where his identity located him in society—a location he had no choice but to contend with.

Believing that one's moral responsibility begins and ends with seeing people as individuals tends to push identity contingencies like these out of view. It pushes us to see people in terms of internal characteristics, or what we imagine their internal characteristics to be. On the last day of George's life, we just see a large, middle-aged Black man in a tank top possibly trying to pass a counterfeit twenty-dollar bill in a corner bodega. We look for things about George the individual that could explain this—poor impulse control, a broader lack of executive self-control, dysfunctional cultural beliefs, deficits in employable cognitive skills. We downplay, or miss completely, the gauntlet of conditions tied to his race and class that he would have had to surmount in order to gain a secure connection to school, the economy, and society.

This blindness lets us see George in decontextualized terms. It's as if the place his identity landed him in society has little relevance to, say, his sense of how important schooling was in light of his family's needs; how he experienced society's evaluative assessments and disciplinary practices; the social capital he had to make decisions about his education; how schools and other institutions like the criminal justice system should respond to him. It leads us to stress the extent to which "grit," or his own agency, determined his life outcomes. And, of course, he and his family did have agency, responsibility, and "grit." There is ample evidence of their exercising these capacities within the opportunities afforded them. But how much "grit" would it have taken for George to have surmounted the gauntlet of conditions society imposed on him based on his identity—from the day he was born to the day he died? At some level we know that different identities experience different realities in society. As the comedian Chris Rock famously put it: "Ain't a white man in this room that would change places with me . . . and I'm rich."

Identity-blindness allows us to treat other people's realities as if they are unreal or irrelevant and thereby allows us to feel less responsibility for addressing them. This is why being on the receiving end of this blindness—for example, being George Floyd and being told by everyone from his teachers to police officers that they are color-blind—can be frustrating. It is difficult to believe and it signals that one is not being seen.

4.

There was an understanding of their early relationship that both Calogero and Jane wanted to trust—that they liked each other. Jane told Calogero that she liked Italian boys. But Calogero couldn't take that claim at face value. He knew his community and her community were at odds. The threat of violence between them was always in the air. It took the door test, something concrete in the immediate situation, for him to trust her, to reduce his churn.

CHURN HAS AN ANTIDOTE

Similarly, there is an understanding of the schools, workplaces, and public spaces of our society that we would like people to trust—that they are basically fair places that offer genuine and *equal* opportunity. But for people like George Floyd, and others whose families and communities have experienced identity-based disadvantages, this proposition can be difficult to trust. Saying that these places are now color-blind doesn't help much. People *remember*. They know that the inequalities that stem from those disadvantages have not been remedied. One look at their still largely segregated schooling opportunities, or an unfortunate encounter with the police, tells them otherwise. And even if these places were now color-blind, are such institutions prepared to address the legacies of prior discrimination? People are likely to take assertions of color-blindness the way Calogero took Jane's assertions that she liked Italian boys—as a well-intended hope for society but, perhaps inadvertently, as a denial of their lived experience—a personal claim of innocence more than a real commitment to a more just society.

Like Calogero, to trust, they would need a more concrete signal, like a gracefully unlocked car door, that tells them that in this setting, that vision of a fair, color-blind society can be trusted.

This book proposes a different strategy for building a successfully integrated society—a focus on building trust that real-life settings can meet the needs of people of all identities. It's a simple idea: When an individual, community, or institution tries to grasp and be responsive to the disadvantaging conditions in people's lives, including those tied to their identity—as opposed to staying blind to them—a trust that spans identity differences can follow. Then we can more easily trust the preferred vision of a setting—a school, workplace, or the larger society—as identity-fair. Churn can fade.

To gain the level of diversity our society now enjoys in schools, workplaces, the media, corporations, and elsewhere, we've had to rely in large part on the force of law and on regulations—*Brown v. Board of Education*, the civil rights acts of 1964 and 1965, affirmative action policies that pressed for greater diversity in our institutions and government contracting (now outlawed in college admissions by *Students for Fair Admissions v. Harvard*), and so on. These laws and regulations placed *outside*, top-down pressure on the settings of society to desegregate. Of necessity, they have been our chief approach to achieving a more diverse society. The struggle to conceive and implement these approaches amounts to one of the most successful and nonviolent transformations of society that I know of, and the gains achieved are significant, notwithstanding the distance we have yet to go. I cannot imagine our having made the progress we've made without them.

This book's interest is to expand this approach to include a focus on mobilizing the settings of society themselves to foster successful integration. It sees these settings as having a capacity of their own, bottom-up, to foster successful integration—a capacity, perhaps underappreciated, to build trust across otherwise tenacious identity divides. It explores how to do this at several levels in society: in personal relationships and mentorships; in midsize settings like classrooms, sports teams, and small businesses; in larger institutions like universities and corporations; and in the overarching paradigms we use to design institutions like K–12 schooling.

5.

I said a lot of this to a friend who had, perhaps unwisely, asked me what I was writing a book about. Growing a bit impatient with my response, he asked a question. What is the advantage of focusing on trust-building rather than what we more typically focus on—changing people's prejudicial beliefs? Wouldn't eradicating prejudice be the more important thing to do? I didn't answer him well in the moment, but later, four things came to mind:

First, it's probably easier, at least much of the time, to build trust in familiar, everyday settings than it is to rid people of lifelong prejudices that are sometimes beneath their conscious awareness—not that trying to do so should ever be less than a foundational mission of education.

Second, as subsequent chapters attempt to show, there are new, evidenced-based ways of building trust in everyday settings that have been shown to reduce or eliminate some of the group performance and outcome gaps that have long plagued our society.

Third, anybody can practice trust-building. You don't have to be the same age, race, or sex as the people you are interacting with or even have a high level of multicultural sophistication. These things can help. But trust-building is a game played on the ground. It's a lot about who shows up, listens, and offers concrete, collaborative help and support—things most of us can do, especially if we understand that this is what we should do.

Fourth, reducing churn may be an especially effective way to reduce prejudice. Decades of research in psychology show that one's attitudes (prejudices) *follow* behavior (discrimination) more than they *cause* behavior. That is, whereas our attitudes are often weak drivers of our behavior, our behavior is often a strong driver of our attitudes—our attitudes often change to fit or justify how we behave more than they *cause* behavior in the first place. For example, if we live segregated lives—the behavior—then prejudicial attitudes will likely arise to justify that segregation. So if building trust and reducing churn enables people to be comfortable with each other in diverse settings—think of the parents and teacher in the opening vignette—the prejudices that justified their separation may fade, replaced by attitudes that justify their coming together.

WITH A SLIGHT NOD OF APPROVAL, my friend asked another question. If this reasoning is correct, wouldn't we have recognized it long ago? "I'm not sure we haven't" was my first reaction. Then I asked him to remember what I noted earlier, that most of our institutions originated during our long history as a racially and ethnically segregated society. It's only in the last seventy or so years that our mainstream institutions have felt a modern-day responsibility to the full diversity of Americans. Our chief response has been to pursue personal prejudice reduction—a necessary effort indeed. But doing so with little remedying of longstanding structural, economic, and social inequalities has come to seem disingenuous. Uninspiring of trust. We need a new approach. It is into this breach that *Churn* steps.

CHAPTER 4

Being Wise, Not Color-Blind

HOW INDIVIDUALS CAN BUILD TRUST ACROSS IDENTITY DIVIDES

1.

Gil Evans and Miles Davis collaborated in the 1940s, '50s, and '60s to produce some of that century's most beautiful jazz—with Davis, the great jazz trumpeter, in classically shaped orchestral arrangements developed by Evans. Warm, richly woven music. Yet by sociological lights, this was an unlikely partnership—Davis, the self-contained cool urban leader of a Black art form with deep sensitivities about appropriation and opportunities for Black musicians, and Evans, in Davis's words, "a tall, thin white guy from Canada," a dance band arranger who came to jazz clubs and ate radishes and salt out of a brown paper bag. Evans gained seamless membership in the world of Black jazz musicians. His partnership and friendship with Davis lasted until his death in 1988, when Davis called him his "best friend" and said, "A person is lucky if he has one Gil Evans in his life."

BEING WISE, NOT COLOR-BLIND

How did Evans jump the chasms of American racial segregation and dehumanizing stereotypes during this era to gain the trust of, and admittance to, a largely Black, racially proprietary world? The answer is that he could see the stigmatization of Black life in that era, and he could also see the artistry and full humanity of the people contending with it. He admired the creativity and brilliance of Black art. He wanted to bring his skills to that table. And while he may have lacked the personal style of Black jazz musicians of that day, he had an authenticity that was recognized and appreciated. This made him, in Davis's terms, "cool." "Gil was so cool," he said. Black musicians trusted him. Having given trust and respect, Evans got it in return. "Gil and I hit it off right away," Davis said.

2.

In the 1950s, Erving Goffman, one of the leading sociologists of the last half of the twentieth century, wrote a classic book on the nature of stigmatization entitled *Stigma: Notes on the Management of Spoiled Identity*. It was informed by gay bar culture of that era in San Francisco. In that period of intense anti-gay bigotry, Goffman learned that the men of this culture had a term for straight people they trusted. The term was "wise," as in "he's OK, he's wise, he knows who we are, he sees us as fully human." Miles Davis's description of Gil Evans tells us that African Americans have similar terms: "he's cool" or "he's hip," meaning, again, that he knows what's up, he knows that racial stigmatization is a real predicament in the lives of African Americans, that it takes intelligence and strength of character to survive it, and that, in cases like Miles Davis's, it can foster great art that reveals the humanity that exists behind stigmatization.

Gil Evans was hip to this. He didn't say that he, Gil Evans, had decided to overlook Miles's racial identity—be blind to it—and through that approach see him as fully human, as "just like everybody else." That would be color-blindness. That would be sweeping aside as irrelevant a huge feature of Miles's life and experience. It might be the view of a person occupying a high role in the Wilkerson play. A person who didn't have to know the names of the people in the chorus. A person not wanting to appear prejudiced, perhaps, but not really wanting to be concerned about the experience of people in the lesser roles. What Evans saw and accepted was Miles's actual experience and how he dealt with it. His affinity for Miles was a knowing affinity. That's what made him "cool" despite his eating radishes out of a brown paper bag in Manhattan jazz clubs.

The rhetorical claim of color-blindness is often offered in defense of a good intention: to not discount someone's full humanity based on their group identity. It's an intention that I appreciate. But it unfortunately implies that one can overlook even profound parts of another person—experiences tied to their group identity—and still convincingly see them for who they are. So for people on the receiving end, it can raise questions: If you don't see my identity or acknowledge the conditions that go with it in this society, how can you see me for who I am? And if you don't see me for who I am, how can I trust you? Can a person or institution so willing to ignore a major truth of my life be trusted?

BEING WISE, NOT COLOR-BLIND

Wiseness sees full humanity *in* human difference. It sees human differences as the way equal humanity manifests itself differently under different life conditions. It understands that different conditions are tied to different group identities in society, to different statuses in the Wilkerson play. And it understands that group cultures evolve to contend with those conditions—Gil Evans understood the extraordinary artistry of Miles Davis as being rooted, in part, in his identity and in the circumstances and culture of the people who shared that identity.

As Goffman put it:

> One type of wise person is he whose wiseness comes from working in an establishment which caters . . . to the wants of those with a particular stigma. . . . For example . . . Gentile employees in delicatessens are often wise, as are straight bartenders in homosexual bars. . . .
>
> A second type of wise person is the individual who is related . . . to a stigmatized individual. . . . the daughter of the ex-con, the parent of the [handicapped child], the friend of the blind.

Or in my case—to the extent I'd hazard a claim of wiseness—it would come, in large part, from experiencing up close the full humanity of parents of different races and different racial subcultures.

Remember, a chief risk of being in a diverse setting is that we can be seen in terms of out-group stereotypes. It's precisely this risk that can make diverse settings more uncomfortable than homogeneous settings. And when those stereotypes are negative and the setting is important, we churn over possible consequences—as did the parents and teacher. The teacher might have said that her school tried to be color-blind. Who could blame her? But the parents could take that as a red flag. It might not quell their sense of threat at all. To do that would require something more: some sign that, in this setting, they are seen and respected for who they actually are. They'd need this because of the worry pressed on them by those stereotypes. They'd need a concrete signal that despite those stereotypes, their full humanity is understood and respected.

This could take many forms. It could be the teacher inviting the parents to join her in a working relationship to support their son. She might express confidence in his potential. She could be specific about her goals for his development and the pathways for getting him there. She could offer regular check-in phone calls. Down-to-earth help like this *is the heart* of wiseness. It shows that she understands and accepts their full humanity and the importance of the situation to them. It disambiguates her intentions, clarifies what she's thinking. The parents can see she's not stereotyping them or their son. They can begin to trust her. Nothing magical or especially sophisticated here. Just real help—real help that kills churn and deescalates emotion.

The parents, too, can be wise: express interest in a working relationship with the teacher; provide useful context on their son; invite her to community functions; bring her supplementary materials; accompany her class on field trips. Render real

BEING WISE, NOT COLOR-BLIND

help. Things that signal good faith and, again, disambiguate intentions.

Why is this necessary? one might ask. After all, why can't the parties just trust each other enough to get on with a constructive conversation? It's because it's a diverse setting. There is history between the parties, and there are stereotypes. The two sides don't know each other well. The conversation is important, and the parties' identities put them at risk of being seen in ways that would be abhorrent to them. It's where the simplest of communication could go awry. It isn't personal. It's not due to something they've done or said to each other. It's due to those ghosts of history and the roles these parties have inhabited in the Wilkerson play. That's why wiseness is critical. It's a road to trust, to lower churn. It's what they need to have the conversation both parties want.

Wiseness can be as simple as seeing people in terms other than how they might be stereotyped—for example, inviting a qualified older person to lead a discussion on new technologies. Or it could be holding a person to high standards in an area where their group is negatively stereotyped—for example, encouraging a strong female math student to take advanced physics or encouraging a talented white American basketball player to persist in elite basketball. These actions have wiseness. That is, in assessing people, in selecting people, in deciding which people to encourage, they see potential in difference, even when that difference involves different statuses in the Wilkerson play, and even when those statuses have been long justified by stereotypes.

And wiseness can be highly rewarding. As Goffman put it, the wise may "find themselves accorded a measure of acceptance, a measure of courtesy membership in the clan." It's a way that individuals—teachers, managers, physicians, CEOs, attorneys, coaches, college presidents—can, through their own behavior, build trust across fraught identity lines.

3.

Wiseness may have other power as well. Seeing potential in difference—sometimes even in people whose capacities may not ever have been recognized—may bring forth achievement in places we'd never expect it.

Imagine you are back in elementary school, let's say the fourth grade, and unfortunately you are among the worst math students in your school, and known to be. That's your reputation, a significant part of your identity in the school. You're assigned a tutor. This has happened before. The first tutor was kind. She explained the problems; explained your errors; repeated the correct reasoning multiple times; praised your correct answers. She understood incentives and reinforcements. But when you got a problem right, you sometimes worried that it wasn't due to your own thinking. You knew your reputation in school. You had no assurance the tutor didn't see you that way too—as a bundle of deficits, a faulty machine she was trying to fix. She seemed not to grasp this; the pressure your reputation put you under, the threat of judgment that you felt could come down on you with the slightest math misstep or frustra-

BEING WISE, NOT COLOR-BLIND

tion. You learned a little. But doing math became an emotional slog. You dreaded it.

The new tutor was different. She was relational, not gushy, but attentive. She intuitively understood you were working under the weight, the history, of a reputation—that it was "in the air," waiting to be validated by your first frustration. She knew that any sign of a lack of confidence in your ability could send you into a churn of self-doubt and very likely kill your interest.

She understood that her job was more than conveying information and instruction. She had to keep your bad-at-math reputation out of view long enough for you to see your own potential—something she had genuine faith in. She also knew she couldn't just tell you to ignore the reputation. That would be her word against your wide reputation. It would be hard for you to accept. Rather, her actions had to *imply* a belief in your potential. She took what my colleague Carol Dweck calls a "growth mindset." It began with her *faith in your potential, despite your reputation*. It began with *wiseness*. She engaged you with challenge. She picked problems captured by that phrase, "at the frontier of your skills." "Now this is level three . . . it's going to get more difficult." Her instruction was Socratic. She wanted you to see that your own thinking could solve problems. She corrected you by asking questions about your reasoning. She inoculated you against frustration. She made it seem normal: "Now, this may be a little harder since it has been a minute since we have done that type of problem." Her praise was largely indirect—"we're ready for the next level of work"—or she reminded you of how hard the problem you solved was—with just a note of being impressed. She diminished your failures; "I think I didn't tell you what I wanted." She used questions to stimulate your curiosity; "OK, can you think of yet another way to solve the problem?" Her questions focused you on solving the small parts of math problems that enabled you to solve whole problems. She avoided any focus on the question of your math ability. She gave no direct praise or criticism of your performance or ability. She used no incentives. She simply led you, in tiny increments, to see your math potential for yourself. You accumulated successes. You became more engaged, more curious, more confident. You began to feel like you could do these problems—your math identity notwithstanding.

Your new tutor's Socratic approach was precisely that used by "expert tutors," as nominated by peer teachers, in a classic study by Stanford's distinguished social-developmental psychologist Mark Lepper and his students in several Palo Alto elementary schools in the late 1980s and early 1990s. (The above quotes are variations on their language.) And it was precisely this kind of tutoring that dramatically improved the math performance of students in those schools who had been doing poorly. (It is an approach that might also help people struggling to learn a sport or a musical instrument.)

The expert tutors recognized the wall of defense that a bad reputation—or "spoiled identity," to use Goffman's term—can put up against learning. They understood that the informational approach of your first tutor sent the wrong signal—that

BEING WISE, NOT COLOR-BLIND

you were being seen through the lens of your bad reputation as in some way problematic, not adequately competent, with a question mark about your potential hanging vividly over your head. As Mark Lepper and his colleagues put it:

> Exactly those things that one would do to present information to students most efficiently about the existence and sources of their errors and misconceptions are, at least for unconfident remedial [reputation-threatened] students, precisely the same things that seem likely to further undermine these students' sense of competence and control.

The expert tutors understood that students' first need was for someone to believe in their potential to learn, despite their reputation. The best tutors understood that students wouldn't learn much without this. They understood the importance of being "wise."

4.

"Wiseness," then, is being able to see full humanity and potential in difference, in people on the other side of an identity divide or on the downside of a bad group stereotype or reputation, and then acting accordingly. For the over-estimators in the Tajfel experiment, this would mean seeing full humanity and potential in under-estimators and treating them with fairness, respect, even interest. At the root of wiseness is an understanding: that, for the most part, identity differences are not categorical, essentialist differences but are different manifestations—usually in response to life circumstances—of a *shared* and *equal* humanity. It sees these differences as rooted more in different conditions of life that groups contend with than in something essential about groups' nature or character. It stresses the equal humanity they share. It's an understanding that renders identity differences less threatening and easier to engage, and invites a learning mindset, a respectful curiosity, toward difference—as a chance to expand one's understanding of the world.

There is of course no assurance that wiseness will always work, that it will always gain the trust of those on whom it is conferred. Still, trust won't likely be earned without it. And it may inspire a reciprocating trust in those who receive it. Remember Goffman: The wise often "find themselves accorded a measure of acceptance, a measure of courtesy membership in the clan." Churn calmed.

Fair enough. But can wiseness work? Can it build trust and reduce churn across a significant identity divide? That is, can this lovely idea stand up to an empirical test?

5.

Geoff Cohen led myself and Lee Ross in a study. We designed an experiment to ask a simple question: How can a white professor give critical feedback to a Black student and have that feedback be trusted? Is there a wise way of doing that? We saw this question as relevant to many types of relationships: manager-employee, doctor-patient, lawyer-client, pastor-parishioner, and so on. We invited white and Black Stanford students into the lab one at a time and asked them to write an essay about their favorite teacher. If the essay was good enough, we told them, we might publish it in a campus magazine we were starting about teaching and learning. We asked them to come back in two days to get feedback on their essays.

The chief measures in the experiment were how much they trusted this feedback and how motivated they were to use the feedback to improve their essays. We varied how the feedback was given. The results, though expected, were unsettling. When we gave the feedback (always a white feedback-giver) either straightforwardly or with a compliment preceding it, Black students trusted it less than white students. Why?

Let's deconstruct. For white students, the feedback indeed seemed straightforward. There was no stereotype "in the air" about their abilities. There was no reason for them to churn, or believe the feedback was based on anything but their essays. But for the Black students—given the history and stereotypes of American society—the feedback could be ambiguous. Was it based on their essays or on the feedback-giver's stereotype-driven view of their group's abilities? It was hard to know for sure... which made the feedback ambiguous and hard for them to trust on the face of it. And trusting it less, they were less motivated to use it to improve their essays.

This finding shows something profound: how stereotypes about an identity that are merely "in the air" can unsettle trust that is critical for learning, or for benefitting from feedback more generally. This isn't a passing predicament. It's something that our Black participants will regularly deal with in diverse schools and workplaces throughout their lives—the attributional ambiguity, as my colleagues Jennifer Crocker and Brenda Major have called it, of not knowing whether critical feedback is warranted or coming from negative stereotypes that are "in the air." It was an expected finding. It fit the reasoning my colleagues and I were developing. But it was nonetheless unsettling to see something so "in the air," so abstract and unspoken, undermine a critical kind of trust that should be commonplace.

On a more hopeful note, the experiment also found a wise way to give critical feedback. In a third condition, the feedback-giver said to each participant that he was using high standards in evaluating their work and that, having looked at their essay, he believed that they had the potential to meet those standards. This signaled to the Black participants that they weren't being stereotyped. If they were, they wouldn't be held to high standards or have their potential affirmed. This feedback was water on parched land for Black participants. They trusted it as much as white students did. And trusting it, they used it to improve their essays. Three times more of them took their essays home to improve than did participants in any other condition of the experiment.

6.

The worry over possibly being negatively stereotyped in an important setting—seen, for example, as less than intelligent (or as racist) based on your identity—is that people will sum you up with those stereotypes and see nothing else about you. Imagine being thus stereotyped and being in a demanding classroom, a place where you are constantly at risk of being seen in terms of that stereotype—a place where the stereotype primes people to see your frustrations as confirmatory and your successes as an exception to its rule. You'd likely be uncomfortable there, distracted by churn, especially when things got difficult. Motivated to prove yourself, you would perhaps find yourself, confoundingly, less able than usual to work or perform well.

But what if you had a teacher with a particular wiseness: one who realized how you felt and who knew that you needed a chance to affirm your promise both to yourself and to others in the setting (especially the teacher) so that they would know who you really are and would know the things about you that reflect what you value most in life? Would this make you less worried about being stereotyped? Would it enable you to trust the setting more? Would it slow your churn and enable you to work and perform better?

Geoff Cohen (again), Valerie Purdie Greenaway,[*] Julio Garcia—former graduate school classmates—and their students Nancy Apfel and Allison Master thought it might. They went to work. In several racially integrated seventh-grade classrooms in the Northeast, at the beginning of the school year, they gave a set of envelopes to each classroom teacher and asked them to set aside fifteen minutes of class time for students to complete the exercise described in the envelopes. Each envelope had a

---

[*] She also wrote under the name Valerie Purdie-Vaughns.

student's name on it and was handed to that student. For half of them, the instructions were to list several things they valued most in life (they wrote about such things as a relationship with a grandparent, their religion, their love of playing basketball, a favorite uncle) and then to write a brief paragraph explaining why this valued thing or person was important to them. For the other half—the control group—the instructions were to list values they *didn't hold* and then write a brief paragraph on why other people might hold them. These control students had a chance to think about values, but not a chance to affirm their own values.

The chief question of the experiment was this: Would the mere act of affirming their treasured values and sharing them with their teacher affect their grades? The research team didn't expect such an effect for white students. They weren't going to school under the weight of a negative stereotype about their group's intelligence. They'd have less need to assert their worth or to be seen, in their teacher's eyes, as deserving. So the affirming of their values shouldn't have much effect on their grades. And it didn't.

But the experience of Black students in this school would be different. They were a minority in the school, had lower levels of achievement, and were thus at risk of being seen through the lens of a negative stereotype about their group's abilities. For these students, the self-affirming exercise significantly improved their grades. They performed better than Blacks who did the non-affirming exercise. And despite the fact that the exercise took a mere fifteen minutes in the seventh grade, the better performance of the affirmed Black students compared to the non-affirmed Black students lasted *all the way through high school*. The initial self-affirmation launched in them a process of increasing resistance to the stereotype: it first lowered their worry about being stereotyped, then they trusted the setting more and experienced less churn; experiencing less churn, they engaged more wholeheartedly in school and performed still better; performing better, in turn, further lowered their churn about the stereotype, which further improved their performance. And so on.

This pattern of findings was replicated in a large sample study (over one thousand students) in eleven Madison, Wisconsin, middle schools by Geoffrey Borman and his colleagues at the University of Wisconsin (Borman is now a professor at Arizona State University). As in the Cohen research, the initial self-affirmation intervention was conducted when participants were in the seventh grade. Also as in the Cohen research, they were followed all the way through high school. The results were presented in three reports—the first published in 2016 and the last in 2021. This research, too, found that the self-affirmation intervention, in its first year, significantly improved the academic performance of Black and Hispanic students in schools where they were lower in number and in level of achievement—precisely the conditions in which their identity threat would be greatest. And again, this effect lasted. From the seventh grade through the last year of high school, the racial achievement gap for affirmed students grew 50 percent less each year than the gap for non-affirmed students. The achievement gap between white and Asian students and Black and Latino students had decreased by 42 percent by the end of high school. And the intervention increased the percentage of minority students eventually graduating from high school on time by 10 percentage points. All of this from a twenty-minute affirmation exercise in the seventh grade! It launched a process of ever-increasing engagement with school that lifted these students' trajectories of achievement. Similar effects have now been replicated in ability-stereotyped groups from Latino students in the United States to immigrant groups in several European and UK schools. Clearly when we're under the threat of being negatively stereotyped, we appreciate an opportunity to tell people who we really are, to tell them that we are more than whatever the stereotype, or the image of our group, says we are. It's "wise" to understand this. Here, then, is another way to build trust across identity divides: Give people a chance to tell you how they'd like to be understood. If I am doing most of the talking in a diverse setting, I'm probably not being "wise." I'm probably not letting others tell me how they'd like to be seen—leaving them to worry that I will see them stereotypically. Leaving them to churn. Giving people a chance to emerge from behind negative stereotypes lessens that need to churn.

CHAPTER 5

Trust in the Face of Power

What Obama was able to offer white America is something very few African Americans could—trust.

—Ta-Nehisi Coates

1.

As I worked on the ideas in *Churn*, I felt certain things were becoming clear: that trust was indeed a critical ingredient of successful diversity in many of the everyday settings and relationships of our lives; that wiseness—seeing full humanity in human difference—was a mindset for winning trust between people of otherwise wary identities; that giving people the opportunity to tell you about their values, their needs, and their own agendas amounted to wiseness and was a usable strategy; that when giving feedback across identity divides, it was especially important to convey faith in the other party's potential; and that follow-through, giving real help in achieving these things, was just as essential.

It wasn't that I believed that these things, even if implemented all together, would always and definitively eliminate diversity tension. Rather, my growing conviction was that they could *reduce* these tensions—provide traction against them—in our relationships and everyday settings and thus expand the approaches we had to address this central American challenge. Still, a question—also raised by several friends and colleagues—lingered. Was wiseness a strategy for everyone? Would people with less enfranchised identities, those occupying lesser roles in the Wilkerson play, be comfortable using it?

For these people—women, minorities, gays, white men in diversity workshops, low-income earners—hearing that they should offer "trust" in diverse settings could trigger more "remembering" than "forgetting." And there waiting for them is a compelling argument: "How can I trust people from groups that have done bad things to my group, people who benefit from advantages won by those bad things, people who often justify those advantages with dehumanizing stereotypes of my group, people who often see my group's progress not as a good thing, or as justice-restoring, but as a zero-sum loss? Wouldn't being 'wise' just make me more vulnerable to them—women to men, Blacks to whites, gays to straights?" And their churn wouldn't stop there. It would also ask: "Why does responsibility for building trust in these settings fall so much to me? Shouldn't it be first the responsibility of the more empowered?"

They might know that there are exceptions. That among the enfranchised in a setting, there are people who would see their humanity, people who would assume a full share of responsibility for building trust, people who are allies. But how can they know who they are? Isn't it smarter to be broadly vigilant, to stay a bit in churn, especially in important settings, especially early on?

Isn't this what the African American Stanford students were doing in the first two conditions of Cohen's experiment on feedback—the conditions in which the feedback on their essays was given straightforwardly or with a broad compliment first? Given in these ways, Black students couldn't be sure the feedback was free of bias. Was it based on the essay they'd written, or was it based on the white feedback-giver's low opinion of their group's abilities? They couldn't know for sure. So, unlike the white students—who had no such concerns about the feedback—they couldn't take it at face value. Color-blindness would ask, "why not?"; color-blindness would discount the significance of their identity in this situation. Color-blindness would say that these Black students are, by all counts, privileged individuals in a university dedicated to their development. Why would they question the feedback? But Black students have lived with their racial identity. They know it can matter. They didn't know that it would matter in this instance. But they knew it could. Thus their predicament. To be safe, not to be misled, they were less trusting. They stayed in churn.

Such caution has its costs. There could be value in that feedback. It might help them with their essay and their writing generally. Trusting less means they'd miss out on that benefit. And this would happen over and over in a diverse school. Most of their instructors, fellow students, and advisors would be white, or non-Black. So unless this school somehow mitigated their churn, they could remain defensive, unstably engaged—in a place that ostensibly offers so much opportunity. It could contribute to academic underperformance, even diminished career ambitions.

Were we their parents, how would we advise them? To "remember"? To stay wary of what they hear from non-Blacks in the setting—their feedback, their advice, their friendship, the opportunities they offer. To "forget"?—to discard their doubts and trust those around them? Or would we advise a middle course: "trust but verify," with perhaps guidelines for verifying? In my experience, these "guidelines" abound in places like Black barbershops:

> "Look at what people do, not what they say."

> "Allow three strikes. The first and second time a situation appears biased, trust it anyway, but the third time, don't trust it—and act accordingly."

> "Beware of people who *go out of their way* to let you know they voted for Obama, or have Black or minority friends. It can be a red flag."

These "rules" help people position themselves on the continuum between trusting too readily (and opening themselves to disappointment) and trusting too slowly (and risking isolation from valuable feedback, relationships, and opportunities).

I'm using examples from African American experience. But unstable trust is not intrinsic to a group. It arises from a group's lower position in the hierarchy of a setting. Imagine, for example, a white male in a diversity training seminar with mostly women, or in a Black history course with mostly African Americans. In many American settings, white males occupy a high position in the hierarchy of groups. But less so in these settings. In these settings they, too, like the teacher in the parent-teacher conference, could worry: "Do I 'forget,' and trust how this remark will be received?" "Do I 'remember' how my group can be seen, and withhold this remark?" "How much can I trust this setting?" Churn like this is what can make diversity uncomfortable.

In answer to the question "Is wiseness—offering trust to beget trust—for everyone?": I'm afraid it's too much to expect from the less powerfully situated in a diverse setting, especially early on. It simply makes them too vulnerable. And it could well seem impossible. In describing what he saw as President Barack Obama's exceptional ability to offer trust to the American public, including white Americans, the African American journalist Ta-Nehisi Coates wrote, "The vast majority of us [African Americans] are, necessarily, too crippled by our defenses to ever consider such a proposition." They might want to trust a particular setting. But for such trust to seem rational—in light of how they know they could be seen—they'd need evidence that their full humanity and potential are normatively accepted there. They'd need evidence that wise behavior—seeing full humanity and potential in human difference and acting accordingly—is normative in the setting—that in this sense the setting itself is wise. Distinctions, it would seem, must be made. As a general rule, for diverse settings to be wise, it's best for the more empowered to move first—the teacher before the students, the manager before the employees, the doctor before the patient, the parents before the children, the minister before the parishioners, white students before the small number of minorities in a classroom, the coach before the athletes, the CEO before the rank and file, the Black professor of African American history before the minority of whites in the class, the board before the organization's administration, and so on. This isn't to leave the less empowered off the hook. At some point they, too, must be wise—able to see full humanity in difference and put their trust in a setting. The point here—considering the identity power dynamics in a setting—is about who goes first in making wiseness a normative standard. The answer is clear: the more empowered. Most often that means the leadership.

The third condition in the Cohen experiment—the one where the feedback was wise—illustrates this. The white feedback-giver is the empowered party and, in this condition, also wise. His feedback reflected his faith in the students' potential. He said he was using high standards. The students could assume he wouldn't say this if he didn't believe in their ability, if he saw them stereotypically as having low ability. He went further. He said he'd read their essay and believed they could meet those high standards. Wow! He saw potential in difference despite stereotypes to the contrary. This frees these students from worrying about his possible bias against their abilities. It lowers their churn. They could take the feedback more seriously—much more seriously.

TRUST IN THE FACE OF POWER

Remember the other feedback conditions in the Cohen experiment—where the feedback was given just straightforwardly or with a compliment first. These conditions delivered useful feedback, but they gave Black students no evidence that the feedback-giver was trustworthy. They were left with that nagging ambiguity: Was it my essay or a bias of the feedback-giver that shaped the feedback? In these two conditions, Black students wanted to trust the feedback, be motivated by it. But there was that ambiguity. They remained in churn, protectively less engaged. Take this ambiguity away—as did the wise feedback-giver—and Black students showed strong trust and motivation. Their capacity to trust and be motivated was there all along. The spark they needed was evidence that the feedback-giver's expectation of them was not limited by the stereotype about their group's abilities. Then they matched the feedback-giver's trust with their trust, wiseness with wiseness.

Power and status differences, then, can frustrate trust-building in a setting. And wiseness can counter that frustration. But for that to happen, it's best that wiseness come first from the top. It's too much to expect the vulnerable to risk further vulnerability by trusting first. (Though this can happen, as we shall shortly see.) Once leadership offers trust, like the wise feedback-giver in the Cohen experiment, it becomes a path the vulnerable can follow. So, the advice offered here is that in diverse settings—be it an interaction between a doctor and her patient, a lawyer and her client, a teacher and his students, an institution and its constituents, a business and its customers—the more empowered identity should lead with trust.

One might ask, then: Does having power make it easier to instill norms of wiseness in a setting? Can it increase the uptake of wiseness?

2.

Imagine you are in a trust game with another person. The games master has given the other person $1 and told him that if he gives the dollar to you, you will be given an additional $2, giving you a $3 kitty that you could split between the two of you. This split would give him at least $.50 more than he would get if he keeps the $1 for himself. But—and here's where the game becomes a game of trust—to do that, to give you his dollar, he has to trust you. He knows that if he gives you the dollar, you could keep it and the whole kitty for yourself. So to give you his dollar, he must trust that you would split the kitty with him. If he doesn't trust you, he could just keep the dollar, securing at least that much for himself. What he does—whether he gives you the dollar or keeps it for himself—tells you whether he trusts you.

In a second round of the game the roles are reversed. You are given a dollar and the other person (the same person you played with in the first round) must wait to see if you will give it to him or not. What do you do? You now know whether or not he trusted you in the first round. Do you give him the dollar— trusting that he would take that dollar, add it to the $2 he will get, and later split the $3 kitty with you—or do you not trust him, and keep the dollar for yourself?

Marlon Mooijman, a social psychologist at Rice University,

had over a thousand people play this game in an experiment conducted online. What he found was clear. When people were trusted in the first round of the game, they generally reciprocated that trust in the second round by giving their partner the dollar—trusting that he would later split the kitty with them. But when they'd been distrusted in the first round, when the other player had withheld the dollar from them, they generally reciprocated that mistrust, keeping the dollar for themselves. Trust begat trust, distrust begat distrust.

But our question is about relative power and status. What happens if you're playing with someone who has more power in the setting than you do? Would his trusting you—giving you the dollar in the first round of the game—be reciprocated? That is, would you give him the dollar when your turn came in the second round? Or would you be wary of his greater power and trust him less? Perhaps his giving you the dollar in the first round was just a ploy to get you to reciprocate in the second round. Then, by getting your dollar in that round, he would get the additional $2 and be able keep the whole $3 kitty for himself—maximizing his take over the two rounds of the game. After all, he had power. He was free to do what he wanted. Paranoid thinking? Perhaps. But plausible enough to possibly undermine any trust you may have felt—and thus your willingness to reciprocate any trust your partner had shown you.

Mooijman's experiment included a condition to test this possibility. Again, imagine yourself playing the trust game. But this time, your partner has more power and status in the setting than you do. Mooijman told participants that their partner had been selected to distribute lottery tickets among the six or so people who were playing the trust game at the same time. (This lottery was worth $135 million at the time.) Your partner had this power. You didn't. And your partner could exercise that power any way he saw fit. So when he trusted you, when he had given you the dollar in the first part of the game, do you reciprocate? Do you give him the dollar when your turn comes? Or, made cynical by his greater power, do you mistrust him and not reciprocate?

The results were clear. Power did not suppress the reciprocation of trust. It amplified it. Compared to playing with a partner of equal power, participants reciprocated trust more when their partner had greater power. They also reciprocated *distrust* more when their partner had greater power. That is, when the partner distrusted them—failed to give them a dollar in the first round of the game—they were less willing to give him a dollar when their turn came. And this effect was stronger when their partner had more power than when he had equal power. Having a powerfully situated partner accentuated the pattern of results found with partners of equal power.

Mooijman didn't stop there. He tested these ideas in four additional experiments. He always found the same thing: People gave trust when they got trust, and distrust when they got distrust. And this tendency was stronger when their partner had more power in the setting. The power relations in these experiments were transitory—not ongoing, as they are in many real-life settings. Still, Mooijman feels they raise an important caution for leaders, managers, and people in more powerfully situated roles in society: "Having power acts like a double-edged sword when it comes to trust development. Trusting others is particularly effective for promoting reciprocal trust, whereas distrusting others is particularly destructive for promoting reciprocal trust."

3.

All of this said, a question remains: Can trying to build trust ever be a viable way for the *less* empowered to gain comfort and acceptance in a diverse setting? As I've discussed, there's good reason to think not. Wiseness can just be too high-risk for the less empowered. Still, can it ever be useful to them?

Ta-Nehisi Coates has an intriguing theory of what it is about Barack Obama that allowed white voters to trust him enough to help elect him president of the United States. He starts by noting how Obama was raised compared to most Black Americans—by a white mother and grandparents in Hawaii, a state less racially stratified than others. Obama told Coates that he "rarely had 'the working assumption of discrimination, the working assumption that white people would not treat me right or give me an opportunity or judge me [other than] on the basis of merit. . . . [That] kind of working assumption . . . is less embedded in my psyche than it is, say, with Michelle.'" Obama, writes Coates, "sees race through a different lens."

A friend of Obama's, Kaye Wilson, told Coates that Obama's lens is "just very different from ours. . . . I think he grew up in a way that he had to trust [white people]—how can you live under the roof with people and think that they don't love you? He needs that frame of reference. He needs that lens. If he didn't have it, it would be . . . a Jesse Jackson, you know? Or Al Sharpton. Different lens." A lens that allowed him, Coates argues, to imagine becoming president.

Coates argues that Obama's wiseness—his openness to trusting white Americans who have a more powerfully situated identity than his own—played a significant role in his gaining the trust of the American people and winning the presidency. "Obama isn't shuffling before white power . . . or flattering white ego. . . . He stands firm in his own cultural tradition and says to the country something virtually no black person can, but every president must: 'I believe you.'" Social psychologists often define trust as "the willingness to be vulnerable to others." In "believing" white Americans, Obama was in essence saying he trusted them. He would believe them when they expressed their needs. He would be "vulnerable" to the responsibility of serving them. In return, he got their trust—and many of their votes.

Obama isn't alone in understanding this. At least among those inhabiting less empowered identities, it may be intuitively understood that to influence more powerfully situated people, one must first gain their trust. A team of social psychologists—Ruth Ditlmann, Valerie Purdie-Greenaway, John Dovidio, and Michael Naft—put this idea to test in an intriguing experiment. They asked pairs of white and Black college students to have a conversation in the laboratory about the best way to teach one of two difficult topics: climate change, and the chattel slavery of African Americans. They found that Black participants were generally more interested in influencing their partners on how the topic of chattel slavery was taught than on how the topic of climate change was taught—probably feeling a greater sense of personal connection to that topic.

In an earlier session, the experimenters measured all participants' power motivation—that is, the strength of their general desire to have an impact, to influence and control. What they found was interesting: The more that Black students desired influence, the more they used warmth and images of affiliation and friendliness to influence their white partners on the chattel slavery topic, the topic they cared most about. They seemed to understand that to have influence on such a fraught topic with their white partner, they needed to build trust. And, as with Obama, it worked. A later study found that white students were more persuaded on the chattel slavery topic, more attentive and relaxed—they churned less—when they received an affiliative message from their Black partner than when they received a non-affiliative message.

So, yes, wiseness can work both ways. It can help the more empowered build trust with the less empowered. It can help the less empowered build trust with the more empowered. Yet the risks that go along with trusting are clearly greater for the less empowered. So again, this book's general recommendation is for the more empowered in a setting to go first in offering trust.

This is practical advice, in service to being realistic about the dynamics of our everyday work, school, and civic settings. But having witnessed transformations of society brought about by disempowered people, I'd feel remiss leaving it there.

4.

Leaving out trust instigated by the less empowered would miss how behaving out of trust—with faith in other people's capacity for fairness—can be its own source of power, even when, or especially when, it comes from people lower in the social order. There is the Obama example. He offered trust from an identity most would consider disempowered—being an African American with a Muslim middle name and relatively little political experience. He is an extraordinarily talented and charming person of the highest character. Yet his having faith in this country's capacity for fairness seemed to have its own role in his ascendance. It seemed to tell people that despite his identities, he could be trusted. His trust in them begat their trust in him. And their trust enabled them to accept, rather than resist, his strengths.

As it turns out, Obama was reading from a playbook with well-worn pages. Before him were Martin Luther King Jr. and John Lewis, who made this idea of initiating trust a foundation of the American civil rights movement. And before them was Gandhi, who made this idea a foundation of the resistance to Britain's colonial rule of India. And before Gandhi, as we shall see, there were still others. Holding on to one's faith in people's capacity for fairness from a disempowered position, and in the face of intense opposition, while saturated with risks, has a moral power capable of moving a presidential election or, for that matter, the soul of a nation.

Consider the historian and journalist Christopher Klein's 2020 report of what happened on March 7, 1965, in Selma, Alabama—the starting point of a fifty-two-mile protest march

TRUST IN THE FACE OF POWER

by six hundred voting-rights advocates to the state capital of Montgomery—and in the broader United States:

> Perhaps no place was Jim Crow's grip tighter than in Dallas County, Alabama, where African Americans made up more than half of the population, yet accounted for just 2 percent of registered voters....
>
> Once Lewis [chair of the Student Nonviolent Coordinating Committee, or SNCC, and future Georgia congressman] and [Hosea] Williams [representing the Southern Christian Leadership Conference] reached the crest of the [Edmund Pettus] bridge, they saw ... [a] wall of state troopers, wearing white helmets.... some on horseback, and dozens of white spectators waving Confederate flags.... the marchers pressed on in a thin column down the bridge's sidewalk until they stopped about 50 feet away from the authorities....
>
> Major John Cloud [of the Alabama state troopers] called out from his bullhorn. "This is an unlawful assembly.... you are ordered to disperse."...
>
> "Mr. Major," replied Williams, "... can we have a word?"
>
> "I've got nothing further to say...," Cloud answered.
>
> Williams and Lewis stood their ground.... the troopers, with gas masks affixed to their faces and clubs at the ready, advanced.... They knocked the

marchers to the ground.... Clouds of tear gas mixed with... screams.... Deputies on horseback... chased the gasping men, women and children back over the bridge as they swung clubs, whips and rubber tubing wrapped in barbed wire....

Television cameras captured the entire assault....

Around 9:30 p.m., ABC newscaster Frank Reynolds interrupted the network's broadcast of *Judgment at Nuremberg*... the star-studded movie that explored Nazi bigotry... to air the disturbing... footage from Selma. Nearly 50 million Americans... couldn't escape the historical echoes of Nazi storm troopers in the scenes of the rampaging state troopers....

Outrage at "Bloody Sunday" swept the country. Sympathizers staged sit-ins, traffic blockades....

Selma galvanized public opinion and mobilized Congress to pass the Voting Rights Act, which President Johnson signed into law on August 6, 1965.

What Americans saw that evening was among the most dramatic displays of wiseness in American history: people in their Sunday best trying to trust in the democratic ideals of a nation that had never trusted them with full citizenship. People willing to be the first movers in building trust, not from a seat of power but from a seat of highest vulnerability. They lost the battle that day. But they moved the sentiments of the American people. They gained their trust. The 1965 Voting Rights Act, brought about in large part by the Selma march, outlawed the long tradition of requiring impossible poll taxes and literacy tests for only Black voters.

Wiseness—an openness to trust even from a disempowered position—was a core tenet of the nonviolent American civil rights movement. It was during my teen and early adulthood years that it resulted in the legislation that undid the legal foundations of Jim Crow's racial and ethnic segregation, an era that had existed in the United States for nearly one hundred years. I distinctly remember feeling, as the legislation was passed, that a door to a different life had been cracked opened. I knew I owed a debt to the wise discipline of that movement.

5.

Political scientists Erica Chenoweth and Maria Stephan looked at a related question: Which has been more effective at producing social change: armed violent resistance or nonviolent resistance? Embedded is a question about trust: Is offering trust in the ultimate humanity of one's opposition, even from a vulnerable position, an effective way of producing social change, and if so, is it as effective as the threat and use of violence?

Chenoweth and Stephan built a dataset of all the mass change campaigns that happened in the world between 1900 and 2006, 323 in all. They divided them into those that were violent in nature (revolutions, insurgencies, coups d'état) or primarily nonviolent in nature (boycotts, strikes, sit-ins, protest marches, stay-aways). They then assessed how effective they were as measured by whether they achieved their stated goals within a year's time and whether there was evidence that the campaigns themselves, rather than concurrent events or other differences between the societies, were responsible for the change. They checked the reliability of their violent-versus-nonviolent classifications against the judgments of experts.

Of course, major social change involves multiple causes as well as many obstacles no matter how it is achieved. Still, what Chenoweth and Stephan found was dramatic. The Selma march and the larger American civil rights movement were not exceptions. Nonviolent campaigns were ten times more likely to be successful than violent ones. They seem better able to inspire trust between people on opposing sides of a divide, reduce the doubting churn that otherwise exists between them, and thus enable more cooperation going forward. As Chenoweth put it in an interview in the *Harvard Gazette* in 2019, "Countries in which there were nonviolent campaigns were about 10 times likelier to transition to democracies within a five-year period compared to countries in which there were violent campaigns—whether the campaigns succeeded or failed."

The Selma marchers, in their willingness to suffer people's inhumanity out of a faith in people's ultimate humanity, had tapped into a less obvious but long understood source of power.

CHAPTER 6

Making School and Work Settings Wise

IIIIIIIIIIIIIIIIIIIIIIIIIIII

1.

I remember sometimes noticing the color of my hands when I sat in seminars in graduate school. As I've described in other writings, I was the only African American in my graduate program in social psychology at The Ohio State University back in the late 1960s and early 1970s. At a conscious level, I felt I was in a friendly place. By that age, and in those times, I knew what racial animus felt like. I didn't feel it in that program. Still, sometimes in seminars I would notice my hands. They'd make me "remember." Who I was. Who they were—my fellow students and faculty. My racial identity. Their racial identity. I churned: If I blew the answer to a question or, worse, asked a stupid question, what would they think?

We were all Americans. I knew they knew the stereotypes about my group's abilities. In those days, psychologists like Arthur Jensen lectured on college campuses to precisely that point—that African Americans' intellectual abilities were limited genetically. In seminars, those abilities counted a lot. And I knew those stereotypes were just sitting there in the American psyche ready to amplify the significance of any weak performance on my part. And this could happen, I also knew, without them being aware of it. I intuitively understood how stereotypes worked. They specified what was normal. My weak performance could confirm a stereotype about African Americans, while my strong performance could be taken as unusual. One's hands, of course, should be beneath notice in such seminars. But the sight of my hands could push me into a churn of "remembering"—even without anybody present doing anything in particular to provoke it.

2.

The legal concept of a "hostile work environment" acknowledges that workplaces can be hostile in their effects on legally protected identities—racial, sexual, religious, sexual orientation, age. If the hostility interferes with performance, there is a legal right to redress. But in defining a hostile work environment, the law stresses the presence of bad actors, people who actively harass someone or discriminate against their identity. My graduate program wasn't anything like that. There was no discrimination, to my knowledge, and certainly no harassment. Still, especially early in my time there, something kept me on edge.

Some years back, the brilliant Latina social psychologist Mary Murphy led a small team of researchers—James Gross, one of the nation's leading emotion scientists, and me—in an experiment to get a closer look at what that "something" might be. She invited male and female science, technology, engineering, and mathematics (STEM) majors at Stanford into the lab one at a time to evaluate videos advertising a leadership conference to be held at Stanford the following summer. Explaining that she was also interested in their physiological reactions to the video, she asked them if she could attach a sensor to their wrist. All agreed.

Half of the subjects were shown a "balanced" video of photographs ostensibly taken at an earlier version of the conference and showing a ratio of one woman for every man. The other half were shown an "unbalanced video"—essentially the same video except that the ratio was one woman for every three men. Male participants who saw the unbalanced video didn't react to the makeup of the conference participants depicted, either consciously or unconsciously. Their physiological reactions were the same to both videos. Given the subtle difference between them (unless one was told, it was difficult to notice), this wasn't surprising.

The results for women were different. Compared to women who watched the balanced video and to men who watched either video, women who watched the unbalanced video had elevated heart rates and blood pressure, and they sweated more. And, as an indication of their preoccupying churn, they remembered fewer incidental features of either the room they were in or of the video itself. These women were math and science majors. They cared about diversity in these fields—where they might spend their careers. So, though hardly aware of the precise woman-to-man ratio in the videos, like a sense that their shoes were too tight, they were upset by the unbalanced video and its implication of gender imbalance at the leadership conference.

What information did the women in Murphy's experiment get from the photos of the leadership conference?

Elizabeth Alexander offers an answer in *The Trayvon Generation*. She describes having frequently visited a conference room at Yale University for over fifteen years as a faculty member and never once noting that the painting at the front of the room of benefactor Elihu Yale, after whom the university is named, included a small brown boy at his feet with an iron collar around his neck linked to a chain. She was shocked by her "delayed comprehension." "I did my work under the matter-of-fact, unproblematized image of an enslaved brown figure at the foot of the most venerated person in the university's history." Yet at the heart of her "comprehension" was a question: How was she "part of this we"? Did she belong? It is a variation on the question that the women in Mary Murphy's experiment had, the question that the white men who shy away from discussions of diversity have, and for that matter the question that the sight of my hands raised for me in seminars.

Material features of a setting reflect society, its history and culture. They signal what's valued—which traditions, values, achievements—and who belongs. Sometimes this is intended. As Alexander goes on to note in the case of monuments. She asks us to think of Stone Mountain in Georgia, depicting the chief leaders of the Confederacy. Four hundred feet off the ground,

MAKING SCHOOL AND WORK SETTINGS WISE

the figures are ninety feet high, larger than the heads on Mount Rushmore. Its construction was begun in the 1920s and after a long delay was resumed in the 1960s, likely in defiance of the desegregation efforts of the civil rights movement. Think of the churn such a monument could cause in African Americans—descendants of those enslaved.

So, yes, settings and their features—before anybody in a setting does anything—can trigger identity threat and churn. Settings have agency of their own, an agency that can be a problem in an identity-diverse society trying to overcome stratification. Many of our settings—corporate boardrooms, waiting rooms, DEI workshops, art galleries and museums, hiking trails, neighborhoods, faculty meeting rooms, classrooms, country clubs, college campuses—have features (from their demographics to pictures on the wall) that can push one or another identity into churn. And this pushing has consequences.

Several social psychologists—Victoria Plaut, Paul Davies, and I—joined Sapna Cheryan in an ingeniously simple experiment to examine these "consequences." The question: Could the incidental, material features of a setting be enough to affect something as important as a person's career interest? We had college students come to the lab one at a time to complete a survey of their "current feelings toward computer science." The experiment varied the clutter in the room where participants completed the survey. For half of them, the clutter consisted of objects that "one might find in the office of a stereotypical computer scientist" or "in the dorm room of a typical computer science geek"—a *Star Trek* poster, comic books, video game boxes, electronics, soda cans, and junk food containers. For the other half, the clutter wasn't associated with computer science at all—a nature poster, water bottles, poster art, healthy snack boxes, coffee mugs, general interest magazines and books.

Sapna's reasoning was this: Computer science is a male-dominated field. Male-oriented clutter shouldn't deter men's interest in the field. But it could affect women. It could tell them they aren't part of that "we." If the incidental features of a setting can have such influence, if they can affect one's feeling about an entire field, then the male-oriented computer science clutter would depress women's interest in computer science yet have little effect on men's interest. This is precisely what happened. Male clutter depressed women's interest in computer science. It had no effect on men's. Again, the agency of a setting; its incidental features alone affecting something as important as women's interest in an entire field.

3.

Imagine you are a high school senior from a working-class family. You just got admitted to an elite university. You're ecstatic. You hit the jackpot. It's a pathway to a secure, maybe economically better life. Your family is ecstatic too, and very proud. But soon worries emerge. Your mother frets that you're moving into a world she's not part of, that she's losing you. Your father frets too. He and your brothers have a gardening business. They always thought you'd be part of it. They need you. You feel the pull of obligation, responsibility. And there are other worries. Will you have the funds to cover the costs of college, not to speak of the cash to socialize with fellow students? Will people react to the way you speak? Do you grasp the norms of this new world? The university tells you to "find your passion," to find your distinctive interest and pursue it even in the face of discouragement from others. It's the ideal of how to be in this new world. But you've been reared to a different ideal—to feel a strong sense of responsibility to family and community. It's who you feel you are. You can't just walk away from those feelings and obligations just to pursue personal goals. The university pushes you to find your calling. Your parents and community want you to get a good job and come home to help. You're in what Nicole Stephens and her colleagues call a cultural "mismatch"—between your home culture and the culture of the institution you are joining.

Could the churn caused by such a mismatch contribute to the national gap in college achievement between middle- and working-class college students, a gap that has existed for decades? Stephens assembled a distinguished team of collaborators—Stephanie Fryberg, Hazel Rose Markus, Camille Johnson, and Rebecca Covarrubias—to take up this question. They reasoned that the gap might stem in part from signals universities send to students about the "right way" to think about their college experience and—often unintentionally— about the kind of people who belong there. They set out to test this logic.

They recruited first-generation college students—the first in their family to attend college—and college students with college-graduate parents, all in their first semester at a large private university. They gave all participants a set of anagrams to solve as a measure of cognitive skills. But before doing the anagrams, participants read one of two letters of welcome ostensibly written by the university president.

For half of the participants, this letter was based on the letter normally sent to incoming students. It stressed four student goals:

a.) learning by exploring personal interests,
b.) expressing ideas and opinions,
c.) creating your own intellectual journey, and
d.) participating in independent research.

It further said, "[Your university] has a tradition of independence: of bold students who assert their own ideas, thoughts, and opinions."

For the other participants, this letter listed goals more compatible with the culture of working-class students:

a.) learning by being part of a community,
b.) connecting with fellow students and faculty,
c.) working together with and learning from others, and
d.) participating in collaborative research.

It added, "[Your university] has a tradition of learning through community—bridging academic study with public service."

When the letter conveyed an individualistic campus culture—

MAKING SCHOOL AND WORK SETTINGS WISE

a culture better matched to that of students with college-graduated parents—those students outperformed working-class students on the subsequent anagram task—mirroring the national trend of students with college-educated parents doing better in college than students from working-class backgrounds. But when the letter conveyed a more collective campus culture—a culture better matched to that of working-class students—those students performed *the same* on the anagram task as students with college-educated parents. The representation of college culture in the president's welcome letter was enough to immediately affect students' cognitive functioning!

This isn't something that just happens in college. Mary Murphy and her research team found another striking example of such an effort in a real company. 3M is based in Maplewood, Minnesota, outside Saint Paul. It once ranked 95th in the Fortune 500 (in 2025, it ranked 174th). It makes Post-it notes and sells everything from adhesives and abrasives to medical and car-care products. It believes that a company culture of innovation is essential to its success. And it believes that a diverse workforce is essential to a culture of innovation. In Mary's words:

> Each year, roughly one-third of the company's sales revenue comes from products developed within the past five years.... According to 3M ... [this is] due to its emphasis on collaboration. In fact, the company is credited with originating "15 percent time"—a program in which all employees are encouraged to

use 15 percent of their time to tackle questions and challenges that have caught their personal interest—all the way back to 1948. (And yes, all employees, not just engineers, get 15 percent time, because, as the company says, they believe great ideas can come from anywhere.)

3M has had great success with diversity. In 2020, nearly 50 percent of its nonproduction workers were women and/or minorities, and nearly 70 percent of its vice presidents and above were women and/or minorities. In explaining this success, Jayshree Seth, 3M's chief science advocate, points to a central cause: *having changed the stereotype culture in the company.* The company came to recognize the off-putting nature of the standing stereotypes about what science is and who does it—the image of the "genius scientist or an evil scientist or a loner scientist." As Seth notes, "If that's not what they [women and minority employees] want to be," it leads them to "disengage from science." To combat these stereotypes, the company began data-driven assessments of company culture, developed strategies and company units to address this culture, and closely monitored its progress in doing so.

Our society has an inherent challenge: Many of its settings still have features that reflect our identity-stratified history and organization. Our schools, workplaces, churches, classrooms, civic organizations, and boardrooms have features that can make it harder for some identities to trust that they are part of the "we" in the setting. Identity-blindness implies that, along with identity itself, these features don't matter much—they can, or should, be ignored. But they do matter—to all of us. Think of being the "only one" or "one of only a few" in any important setting—as my hands reminded me, for example: one of only a few whites in a Black history seminar, one of only a few Blacks in a symphony orchestra, or one of only a few women in an advanced math course on Riemann surfaces. But there's good news: as the Stephens experiment and the 3M company show, when these features are addressed, improvements can happen, sometimes without much effort or cost. Even a letter of welcome can help.

4.

But how do you go about identifying and addressing the identity-threatening cues in real-life settings? Here is a method, and then an elephant-in-the-room conundrum that can plague these efforts. And what to do about it.

As to method, Mary Murphy and her colleagues have developed a deft and usable approach they call a "cues audit." In settings like corporate divisions, academic departments, nonprofit organizations, boards, classrooms, small businesses, and churches, do three things.

First, educate. Explain how features of settings—the proportion of different identities in the setting; the pictures on the wall; the references people use in their speech; the style differences in people's clothing; the language people use to designate different identities—can cause churn in some people while going unnoticed by others. Point to specific features.

Describe how they can be interpreted differently by different people. It can sometimes be hard for people not implicated by a feature to understand its effect on those who are implicated by it. These differences, however, can often lead to revelatory discussions.

Second, ask people to identify features in a setting that imply that some identities belong there more than others, or that expectations are higher for some identities than for others. These can be collected anonymously in advance of a session in which they are discussed. This can be a revealing exercise. It can pick up features that signal class distinctions—a manager who goes on about his European cathedral tour at staff meetings with people who've never gone to Europe and who have to stay home for their vacations. It can pick up features that signal the dominance of one cultural perspective—a constant stress on the importance of independent achievement over responsibility to community, for example. It can pick up an off-putting diversity philosophy—for example, a gratuitous stress on concepts like white guilt or color-blindness. It can pick up cues that link success to being a certain kind of person—for example, pictures on the wall that link STEM success to being male. It can pick up an overuse of terms like "genius" that suggest critical skills are innate and perhaps not evenly distributed over identities. And so on.

Third, through group discussion, develop plans for addressing the ill effects of problematic cues. This could mean eliminating some cues, developing a better understanding of other cues, modifying cues. And then evaluate the effect of whatever changes are made on people's sense of belonging.

5.

Experience can tell us important things about how to make good ideas work—for example, that *how* something is done can be as important as *what* is done. A cues audit can yield information that is invaluable to the life of a setting. Look at how dramatically it changed 3M. But experience with such efforts tells us something else too: to avoid a heavy hand in implementing it. It shouldn't become a tyranny. I suspect you know what I'm saying. We shouldn't use relatively small violations of emerging mores to morally condemn or socially ostracize a person—to "cancel" them. Terms or behavior that degrade the humanity of other groups—mortal sins—have to be off-limits. But experience suggests it's wiser to treat venial sins with more latitude. Reacting too strongly to them can undermine the very goal we're after—a setting with a climate of greater trust and lower churn. Remember the manager who keeps talking to his staff about his European cathedral tour when many of them can't afford an out-of-town vacation. If this insensitivity is pointed out to him in public, he could, in the immediate situation, explode into defensiveness. And over time, feeling that he has lost stature in the setting over something he regards as an innocent action, he could become an opponent of diversity efforts altogether, framing them as "woke" violations of his freedom of speech. A possible ally of the effort is lost, while the climate of the setting remains in churn.

In the late 1950s and early 1960s, the leadership of the American civil rights movement had a similar concern of retaliatory violence as their marches and protests moved forward. But another concern was *how* they should protest, and how the kind of society they wanted to achieve should shape their protests. In answer, Martin Luther King Jr. borrowed from Josiah Royce (1855–1916) the construct of the "beloved community"—in which people live as brothers and sisters, recognize their interdependence, and act with compassion for one another across identity lines.

For King, this kind of society, this kind of America, was the goal of the movement—with redemption and reconciliation triumphing over retaliation. It was this endgame image that underpinned King's uncompromising commitment to nonviolence. Violence, he believed, would destroy the possibility of such a society. In the founding documents of the Student Nonviolent Coordinating Committee, an arm of the movement that organized the Freedom Rides and the Mississippi voter registration drives, the religious historian Charles Marsh describes how SNCC drew from this concept: "Only 'redemptive community' could supersede 'systems of gross social immorality' and nurture an 'atmosphere in which reconciliation and justice' [become] actual possibilities."

The workplaces, schools, classrooms, laboratories, departments, and public spaces of contemporary society face a similar

MAKING SCHOOL AND WORK SETTINGS WISE

challenge of integrating people of different identities into communities in which differences enrich rather than undermine their functioning. The concept of "beloved community" is perhaps too dated for contemporary use. But it does point to the value of keeping the endgame in mind: achieving a climate in these places in which our identities—the full breadth of them—feel safe and like they can belong and flourish. This is of course still a central challenge of American life. And that is why the image of the endgame should shape the ways we build trust and lower churn in the settings of our society.

This is why I like Mary Murphy's stress on making a system of evaluating the features of settings an educational effort. In that regard, two general guidelines might be useful. First, it should be a low-key, routine practice that, for the most part, focuses on incremental changes that are well integrated into the functioning of a setting. It shouldn't be done once and forgotten. Nor should it be done only when a crisis has arisen. It should be a recurring, normalized activity—part of the operational woodwork. It should also enable the kind of tracking and data collection that would hold changes accountable to evidence: Do they work with regard to important outcomes?

Second, these efforts should involve the participation of as many people as possible. When people feel they haven't been heard, they tend not to trust. But when their input is a regular, normalized part of how a setting functions, they're better able to trust it even when they disagree.

The aim is to establish a practice that keeps people in touch with each other's experience of the setting. An advantage of locating such an effort in specific settings is that that's where trust-building changes are often most feasible and their outcomes most measurable. It enables a culture in which change is empirically driven (see the next chapter for a superb example) and takes place at a pace that is more evolutionary than revolutionary—both features of which foster stability and trust.

Settings of moderate size are one thing. But what about larger institutions and organizations? Can they, too, be made wiser?

CHAPTER 7

Making Institutions Wise

1.

My freshman year in college was frustrating. The only good grade I got all year was an A in introductory psychology—perhaps a harbinger of things to come. Otherwise, it was mostly C's, even a D. I'd gone to a high school of over five thousand students in Harvey, Illinois, a largely industrial town off the South Side of Chicago. My family lived in the adjoining, largely African American, low-income town of Phoenix, Illinois (the median income in Phoenix in 2025 is just over $24,000 per year). I loved reading, but my high school counselors and teachers assumed that most students, especially we African Americans, would work in the surrounding factories after graduation.

I was an athlete, a swimmer, despite this being a rarity for African Americans (in my case being the product of the YMCA system). To the extent that I had achievement motivation in those days, it was about swimming. In the summer before college (and two summers thereafter), I worked at South Chicago Packing Company, then a large meatpacking company in the bowels of the stockyards, to help pay for college. None of this prepared me well for the small, rural, largely white liberal arts college I would attend that fall—Hiram College, in Ohio. It was my mother's alma mater, and its academic demands were substantially new to me at the time. I thought I was working hard. But I remember worrying: "What does it take to succeed here?" I was genuinely confused—in a cloud of ambiguity. And, as one of only eight African Americans in a student body of nine hundred or so at the time, that ambiguity had a certain toxicity: Like Mirna on the trail, I worried that how people saw my race could affect how they saw and treated me. I couldn't rule out that possibility. I was knee-deep in churn.

Good fortune came my way in the form of my sophomore roommate, Pat Neal, who'd grown up in the one-stoplight town of Garrettsville, just five or so miles down the road from Hiram. Garrettsville was the big-city destination for we Hiramites. Pat was one of the "smart kids" at Hiram, with top grades to prove it. By this time, I knew two things: first, that my survival at Hiram was questionable, and second, that I didn't like that. I wanted to succeed there. Images of the alternative—packing beef kidneys and the like in the Chicago stockyards—stiffened my resolve.

I made several decisions. I quit the swim team. I'd done well enough my freshman year, but it took huge amounts of time.

Next, I decided to imitate, in detail, the ways that Pat went about being a student. For example, the way he read a textbook chapter. I'd been laboriously going through chapters line by line, underlining nearly every other sentence with a yellow highlighter. It took forever. And, as my grades reflected, I wasn't retaining much. Pat said don't do that. Instead, skim the chapter first, in twenty minutes or so. No yellow underlining. Then quickly skim it again to grasp its outline. Then read it at a natural pace. That way, its facts and ideas have an outline structure, a narrative, to attach to. Later, recalling the narrative helps with recall of the facts and ideas. A fourth reading, if necessary, consolidates your understanding enough so that you can easily answer essay questions, or handle Socratic questioning in class.

This was transformative advice. I follow it to this day with grant proposals, research articles, and dissertations. Pat also tried to do this reading before the class lecture on the material—a revelation to me. After the lecture, he'd rewrite his notes. With a swimmer's discipline, I followed him to a tee. By the time midterms rolled around, I hardly had to study at all. My grades improved dramatically—all A's that first quarter after my transformation. With just a note of "let's see if this holds up," my parents were impressed. But it did hold up. School had become more interesting and engaging. I was on a different path.

Something else happened too. My churn receded. It didn't vanish. I didn't totally "forget." That's not likely in a society so organized by race, especially in the mid-1960s. But my churn relented considerably. I was more comfortable with fellow students, with faculty. I have puzzled about this. Pat Neal's strategies did nothing to convince me that I wasn't at risk of bias in this environment. So why did I feel less pressure?

A simple experiment is relevant here. Social psychologists David Glass and Jerome Singer got interested in how New Yorkers coped with the stress of living in New York City—the loud noise, dense traffic, the time pressure so often involved in getting around, the sheer complexity of the city. They developed a laboratory analog of city stress. They exposed people to loud noise, then measured their reactions—psychological and physiological—to see how much stress it caused. Half of the participants were given a way of coping: a red button on their desk that they were told could lower the noise. The other half experienced the noise with no red button, no way of coping. By this time, the literature was clear on a major point: the mere knowledge that one has a way of coping with a stressor can reduce its impact. That's how Glass and Singer reasoned New Yorkers got through the day in New York City. They believed they had ways of coping with its stressors, and the belief rendered them less stressed. That's exactly what happened in the analog experiment. Having the red button lowered participants' stress reactions to the noise compared to those who had no button. Yet they rarely pushed it!

Pat Neal's tactics were my red buttons. They didn't refute the threat of bias. If he'd said that, I wouldn't have believed him. Rather, they reduced my operational ambiguity and frustration in the setting. And it was in part this ambiguity that kept me churning about people possibly evaluating me through the lens of race. The new study habits I'd learned from Pat gave me the same sense New Yorkers have about their stresses: that I knew what to do. I knew how to cope. The ambiguity lessened. My frustration lessened, and with it my sense of being under threat. A weight of race was lifted, even though Pat's help had nothing directly to do with race.

How does this work? one might ask. How would reducing my ambiguity about how to cope with the demands of college also reduce my sense of being under identity threat at college? How are these two things connected?

My answer begins with a reminder: Not coping well with a situation that is important to one's future is stressful for anyone. Think of the transition from middle school to high school, or from high school to college. Think of joining a corporation or moving into a military unit or joining an athletic team or even moving to a new town. Transitions often involve ambiguity over how to cope effectively in the new setting. They instigate in all of us a search for what the challenges are, and for how best to meet them. But for those negatively stereotyped in the setting, this search has an extra consideration. It inevitably raises the possibility that they may face bias—devaluation, low expectations, little tolerance for error, little willingness to be associated with—and then the further worry about how to cope with all of this. Something as simple as ordinary coping ambiguity in an important new setting—something everyone faces—can push people negatively stereotyped in the setting into a weightier, more emotion-laden churn.

What happens if one short-circuits these reactions by resolving the predicament that spawned them—by doing for people what Glass and Singer did for their subjects experiencing intense noise? Suppose you give them red buttons, the understanding and responses they need to function better? And suppose you do this early on, even before they enter the setting, and then remind them of these things when they get in trouble—when their performance slips or when they are frustrated?

Preparation and support like this reduce everyone's ambiguity about how to cope and in turn help everyone function better. And for those worried about being stereotyped in the setting, this better functioning makes the stereotype less plausible, less applicable. It makes the ambiguity they face less toxic. At Hiram, after Pat Neal's help improved my performance, I worried less about being stereotyped. I was doing fine—less need for worry.

Also, as with Pat Neal's help, this strategy doesn't depend on convincing people that there's no bias in the setting—something that can be difficult to do. Rather, it lets them feel less susceptible to the threat in the air tied to their identity.

Could this be an additional strategy for integrating our society's organizations and institutions? Give people the red buttons they need to reduce ambiguity about how to cope in the institution. Give them an understanding of the institution and its infrastructure. Give them the social and cultural capital needed to understand the value of the experience. Give them tools and resources. Show them pathways forward. It can seem like an unusual approach to integration or diversity. But remember, *it's ambiguity over how to cope in important settings that virtually forces people facing identity threat to "remember," to worry that bias is a source of their frustration and discomfort. For them, it's an unavoidable part of trying to figure out what's wrong, what's not working in a setting.*

Suppose an entire institution took this approach. What if a university, for example, tried to do for its students what Pat Neal did for me? Would it—by giving students red buttons and reducing toxic ambiguities—improve student outcomes? Would it reduce those group performance and life outcome gaps that have haunted these institutions, and indeed society as a whole, ever since "integration" in the 1960s?

2.

Georgia State University (GSU) is a large public research university spread over seven campuses in Atlanta. It serves fifty-two thousand students—many of whom are low-income, African American, Hispanic, Asian, and first-generation students who enter college with suboptimal K–12 backgrounds and, it would be fair to say, less of the cultural capital needed to navigate a complex university. Throughout much of its history, Georgia State was a commuter college. It served the needs of Atlanta's downtown business community. In the 1960s, things began to change. It accepted its first African American student for a summer school course in 1962. The expansion of the city of Atlanta and its surrounds in the 1960s increased the region's demand for higher education. And a tight academic job market at the time allowed GSU to build a strong faculty. In the next decades it acquired the hallmarks of a full American university—dormitories (developed in partnership with Atlanta's preparation for the 1996 Olympics) and a football team playing in the old Atlanta Braves stadium.

Still, by the early 2000s, like many large public universities with low-income minority communities nearby, it had a problem: low graduation rates. Indeed, this is a national problem. State legislatures everywhere worry about it. In fact, there is a national organization to raise awareness of it—Complete College America. Georgia State's version of it was as bad as any. Enter Timothy Renick, who'd come to Georgia State in the mid-1980s after receiving his PhD in religious studies from Princeton. Raised near the wealth of Great Neck, Long Island, Renick was nonetheless a working-class son whose father was a career military officer. He got into Brown University and graduated with a strong academic record, all the while working multiple jobs and feeling a bit like an outsider—a feeling that stayed with him during graduate school at Princeton. He found his first faculty appointment in philosophy and religious studies at GSU especially gratifying. His background had given him an orientation. And here was a place that fit that orientation. He could serve lower-income students pursuing the promise of the American Dream—students like himself on whose lives he felt he could have an impact.

After decades of sending GSU students on to lofty graduate programs like the one he'd attended—Harvard, Yale, Oxford, Cambridge—he was appointed associate provost for enrollment, registration, and financial aid. To this role, he brought his own orientation. In a recent conversation, he illustrated what that meant. As a teaching assistant at Princeton, one of his students plagiarized his *entire* term paper. Renick had to report it. An extensive adjudication followed. The student brought in lawyers to represent him, pastors to attest to his character. In the end, little happened: perhaps a requirement to rewrite the paper, a warning. But no suspension. Nothing that would derail the student's progress.

In contrast, in Renick's early years at GSU he knew of several low-income students who were dropped from school for not meeting only one small bureaucratic requirement, never to be heard from again. These kinds of experiences brought Renick to an important insight: Academic ability was rarely the reason low-income students dropped out of college. It was mostly little things, potholes along the road to graduation. As Andrew Gumbel put it in *Won't Lose This Dream*, his compelling book describing the transformation of GSU: "Contrary to conventional wisdom, academic performance was not the most important predictor of student success or failure."

Renick believed less in the standard predictors of college success and more in what colleges themselves did to facilitate or hinder that success. Especially for low-income students. It was a different positioning of an institution of higher education. A "wise" positioning. In his view, higher education, in addition to being a *selector* of academic promise—as reflected in schools' use of SAT scores as a factor in admission—should be a *developer* of academic talent, as reflected in the first plank of GSU's Strategic Plan: "to become a national model for undergraduate education by demonstrating that students from all backgrounds can achieve academic and career success *at high rates* [emphasis added]."

Large bureaucratic institutions like universities and corporations are notoriously difficult to change. The reasons range from tradition to weak governance. Renick and his deputy Allison Calhoun-Brown, a soft-spoken political science professor, came to realize the value of data.

In the same way that wise feedback can foster trust in relationships between individuals of different identities, or attention to the features of a setting can foster trust in moderate-sized settings like diverse classrooms, institutional data and data analytics can foster trust in a process of changing large, diverse organizations. Better than the naked eye, these can help identify the potholes and derailments that cause dysfunction, undermine trust, and spread churn throughout an institution. They provide a relatively objective basis for designing and evaluating remedies for those potholes and derailments. And they can provide a relatively objective basis for ongoing decision-making and for recommending change to colleagues and leaders. That is, they can help build trust in the process of change. They lower the churn that could otherwise bring change to a stop. Renick and Calhoun-Brown (as well as Mark Becker, the GSU president who helped launch the transformation) realized that the administration could use data to help their institution change.

Nearly all of the transformations at GSU followed a pattern: A review of institutional data reveals a problem, and then data is used to understand it, design solutions, evaluate small-step interventions, and develop and evaluate university-wide scale-ups. Data is also used to manage the often turbulent political waters of persuading colleagues of the need for change and to gain their support. As Gumbel put it: "This was a strategy that would come to define the entire trajectory of Renick's student success work: start small, show the benefits, then scale the program university-wide." The approach is not "you have to adapt to us" but "we have to adapt to you," said Darryl Holloman, dean of students and vice president of student affairs from 2012 to 2018. As a strategy for institutional change, it inspires trust at every turn.

3.

As a first-year student at GSU, you'd be asked to show up early—seven weeks before school starts. In those weeks you'd join a community of other students learning about virtually every aspect of the institution. There'd be a special focus on navigating curriculum and developing career choices, and on tools and resources available to you to stay in good academic and financial standing at GSU. You'd learn about a Scholarship Resource Center that, for example, has redesigned traditional financial aid packages to offer "retention grants": microgrants of a few hundred dollars or so to help students deal with financial challenges—unpaid tuition and fee balances, car repairs, a mother's lack of rent money—that might otherwise keep them out of school. You'd get financial literacy training. It uses predictive analytics to identify when you and your family will be most at financial risk and helps you develop mitigating strategies. This is real help with the real-life needs of a student body that is nearly 60 percent Pell Grant–eligible, meaning their families have an annual adjusted gross income of $30,000 or less (single parent) or $75,000 or less (two parents). It's help that goes a long way, as you begin your schooling, to clear away financial ambiguities that would otherwise haunt your schooling and perhaps your life thereafter.

You would learn about a Student Advisement Center (SAC) and its computer platform (developed by the Education Advisory Board). It's a platform that accesses student information systems to track performance and class attendance. You would learn that it's used to implement a system of eight hundred alerts—configurations of performance and attendance that data analytics has shown to be trouble signs—and that each alert triggers SAC advisors to reach out to you and play the Pat Neal role: offer help, understanding, and coaching before a problem gets out of hand or before you veer from a course sequence that is best for your goals. Even one bad quiz, in a critical course, can trigger an alert. Advisors then have forty-eight hours to respond—as Renick said, to "call the student in, sit down and meet face-to-face to try to help with whatever they can." In 2014–15, as the system reached full capacity, it generated forty-three thousand meetings between students and their mentors.

SAC also uses data analytics to identify the best and least expensive curricular pathways for your career goals. It even has a chatbot, developed to help students get quick answers to logistical questions about campus life in the summer before they first arrive on campus. It significantly reduced GSU's "summer melt"—the number of admitted students not showing up in the fall. Now it's being expanded as a resource for all students.

Talk about ambiguity reduction and support! But does it work—this clearing of paths, building of cultural capital, intervening at the first sign of trouble? And does it help especially the identity-threatened? Is it a model for how a diverse institution can work?

Yes. Dramatically so. On a campus with so many low-income students, the overall six-year graduation rate in 2003 was 32 percent. In 2024, it was 52 percent. What about toxic ambiguity? If it especially affects the more negatively stereotyped, you'd expect the ambiguity-reducing effects of these efforts to cause the greatest improvements among African American and Hispanic students. In 2003 the graduation rate for African Americans was 29 percent—only 18 percent for African American males. For African Americans in 2022, the graduation rate was 55 percent! For Hispanic students, the gains are even greater. In 2003 their overall graduation rate was 22 percent. In 2024 it was 58 percent. In a society where the percentage of these groups with college degrees in 2023 was 50.2 percent for whites, 27.8 percent for Hispanics, and 34.2 percent for African Americans, Georgia State is a striking engine of upward mobility and an advantage-equalizing force for traditionally less enfranchised students. Importantly, this was done with a reallocation of resources more than with additional resources, and it was driven less by theory than by careful attention to data.

I asked Renick to reflect on these successes. I asked first about GSU's elimination of group differences in graduation rates. He pointed first to diversity itself. The campus population is made up of multiple groups—Blacks, whites, Hispanics, Asians, low-income students. Identity differences are ordinary on campus. Normalized. Not a charged fact of life there. He also stressed that no student success programming is targeted at any specific group. All supports were for all GSU students. He said that Black, Hispanic, and low-income students do trigger more alerts and get more financial assistance than middle-class white students—reflecting group differences in background preparation and family resources. But because these supports are available and used by everyone, they're not seen as based on race or ethnicity—something he feels could be stigmatizing. Renick feels that such normalization helps minority students have a strong sense of belonging. In fact, he has met students who are surprised to learn, after talking to friends at other universities, that these supports aren't available at all colleges.

I asked Renick about student participation in STEM courses—an area where diversifying student and faculty ranks has been especially difficult. He beamed. The data shows that over the history of student success programs, participation in STEM courses has increased, especially that of Black students. It's due to early alerts and well-timed interventions, Renick feels. For example, if students get into a course over their head—an experience that, if left unaddressed, can cause undermining levels of frustration—they can be steered out of it (before getting a poor grade) and into a course sequence that first builds foundational skills. All in a timely fashion. Frustration preempted.

As our conversation ended, Renick left me with an analogy. He said that when faculty at other schools hear about GSU, they sometimes say things like: "Listen, I learned to navigate college on my own. I learned important things that way. Are you sure these wraparound supports are a good idea in the long run?" When he hears this, he asks them to think about preparing their income tax returns. For most, the intricacies of tax law are outside their field. Perhaps they could learn. But the stakes are high, and most choose to get expert help. Renick says GSU students are not in a dissimilar position. Eighty percent have significant jobs, many have family responsibilities, and very few have been prepared to navigate college. Like the tax consultant, he's giving his students needed guidance and providing expertise born of years of such counseling. His results show the transformation that expertise can help to bring about.

GSU is not alone. A ten-member University Innovation Alliance has committed to exploring its data-driven strategies. Also, GSU has its own National Institute for Student Success, headed by Renick, that helps regional public universities use this approach. As the degree of implementation progresses in these schools, graduation rates have increased, sometimes dramatically so, especially for low-income and minority students. And there is another sector of American higher education that, in taking a more developmental approach to its students, has long used its own versions of GSU-type supports: historically Black colleges and universities (HBCUs). Consider Xavier University in New Orleans. It's a school of only 3,300 students. Yet it is among three colleges nationwide that produce the greatest number of Black graduates who go on to apply to US medical schools each year—largely through a rigorous, structured set of practices that give wraparound support and help focus the undergraduate experience.

One thing GSU's success demonstrates is that similar strategies can work in diverse settings as well.

Information. Social capital. Timely intervention and support. A structure outlining clear expectations. These reduce the ambiguity that can become toxic by expanding churn into mistrust and alienation. They foster success for everyone. But they especially help those under stereotype-driven suspicion of not belonging. They reduce performance gaps between these and other groups. They foster a successful form of diversity, even when they don't directly address diversity at all. For example, in the years since the GSU student success programs reached maturity, GSU has reliably produced more African American graduates than any other college or university in the nation.

Still, one might ask: Would these strategies generalize to institutions where student needs are not as dire? Would they be helpful, for example, at a strong graduate school that provides students a living wage, rendering them less financially stressed than undergraduates whose education is funded in part by Pell Grants?

MAKING INSTITUTIONS WISE

4.

Marissa Elena Yáñez, a Latina PhD in bioengineering, got her degree at a large public university. She got through that program in fine order, meeting all of its benchmarks. But it took her a long time, longer than most other students. And it exacted a heavy emotional toll. Her program had very little structure: few markers of progress, vague performance expectations, few signals about the appropriate pace of work, little information about professional opportunities, and little faculty feedback. She felt blanketed in ambiguity. It made it difficult for her to trust that she wouldn't be seen stereotypically. Like me in my early Hiram days, she lived knee-deep in churn. Was she doing enough? How was she being seen? Was sexism or ethnic bias at play? Would she have to work doubly hard to prove herself? Did she belong? Was she an imposter? Nothing in the setting helped her rule out these possibilities. Her response was over-effort. She repeated her experiments over and over when other students would have submitted them for publication. She wanted to be sure. She even delayed submitting her dissertation. Again, repeating the experiments over and over. She was reluctant to apply to conferences and, ultimately, for academic jobs. Her time in graduate school was weighted with emotion that suppressed her ambition, that told her a life as a faculty researcher, for example, would be just more of the same stress. So much of her life had been dedicated to scientific research. Yet upon finally getting her PhD, she sought a life outside of research.

As an aspiring chemist, if you were fortunate enough to be

admitted to the graduate program in the College of Chemistry at the University of California at Berkeley, you'd be asked, just like GSU students, to show up early for school, three weeks early. In those three weeks, you'd be reminded of what you already knew: that students are held to a high standard. It's one of the top three graduate programs in chemistry in the nation. But you'd also learn that your admission means that the faculty believes in your potential to meet those standards. The ambiguity you might have had about this—as many entering graduate students have—begins to clear away.

Then you'd be given critical pieces of cultural capital. For example, you'd learn that success in graduate school is less about course grades than research productivity and publishing—being less a consumer of knowledge, as you were as an undergraduate, than a producer of knowledge, a contributing scientist. You'd learn that this is what you should be about in graduate school. You'd learn it right away. It wouldn't take you months or years of trial and error. This orientation reduces the ambiguity that, as noted, for students whose abilities are negatively stereotyped in the larger society, could become toxic in this setting. More ambiguity cleared away. Then you'd be given a clear expectation: You are to publish your first research article by the end of your first year. It's expected of everyone; no waffling. And to get that ball rolling, you'd meet with as many as three faculty members who would describe their research and identify possible projects for you to get involved in immediately. You'd pick one, or develop another research idea, and immediately meet with the relevant faculty member to develop a plan for doing and publishing the research. To further remove ambiguity about an expected rate of progress, you'd set deadlines for the phases of the research: a research proposal due by, say, November 11; completion of the proposed research by, say, March 3; and a write-up submitted for publication by, say, June 2. More ambiguity removed. And to support you on this path, the faculty supervisor of your project would meet with you every week—to help out and to track progress. And that advisor would be regularly queried by a college-level committee as to your progress and needs. You'd be consistently encouraged by the faculty to publish—as much if you were a woman or minority as if you were a white man, an evenhandedness that, as we shall see, doesn't always exist in STEM graduate programs.

So, you'd begin graduate school with many of its ambiguities resolved. Faculty expectations and their belief in your ability to meet them would be clear—early on. You'd know what accomplishments are most valued in the setting and at what pace you should achieve them. You'd have a concrete project to work on that you knew the faculty approved of. You'd have a specific plan to follow in completing that project with work deadlines precisely specified. You'd be explicitly encouraged by faculty to publish. You'd have faculty support to help with the research and to keep you on schedule. And you'd know that there was some level of faculty accountability for your progress. As Douglas Clark, the college dean, put it: "With this level of structure and given the nearness of deadlines right from the outset, students don't have a lot of time for churn." Does it work?

A team of researchers led by Rodolfo Mendoza-Denton found that it did. They surveyed students' publications and progress toward publication in UC Berkeley's graduate programs in math, physics, astronomy, computer sciences, earth and planetary sciences, and of course chemistry. How well were these programs performing, and were they performing equally well for all groups of students? Were women and underrepresented minorities doing as well as white and Asian men regarding publication? That is the coin of the realm in graduate school and the sciences more generally. They found what they had feared: In all but one of these programs, women and minorities were not publishing or progressing toward publication as quickly as men. The one exception was the College of Chemistry.

The survey offered an explanation: In addition to not meting out encouragement to publish as evenhandedly as the College of Chemistry, the other programs lacked many of the ambiguity-reducing structures implemented in Chemistry. To be clear, the other programs are extraordinarily strong. At the time of the survey, Berkeley had the second-highest number of science departments ranked in the top five nationally. Weaker science wasn't the cause of their weaker performance with women and minorities. Nor did it reflect a lack of interest in seeing all students succeed. The cause seemed to be a lack of ambiguity-reducing structures and practices. Other programs surely had some of these elements. But not all of them. And perhaps not as well coordinated as those in Chemistry.

And part of the reason for this? Marissa Yáñez. After she

got her PhD in chemistry, the non-research life she sought was to help other chemistry graduate students have a better time in graduate school than she'd had. She became the chief diversity officer for Berkeley's College of Chemistry, where she helps administer the churn-reducing structures and supports that she wishes she'd had when she was in graduate school. For her, the options for women and minority graduate students in chemistry—students who will inevitably endure the pressure of negative stereotypes about their group's abilities—are clear: It's either structure and supports or . . . the pain and churn of the imposter syndrome.

There is, of course, another pedagogical mindset in graduate education: Give students the freedom to find what they care about, a true passion that will sustain them as their careers unfold. In this mindset, it's reasonable to rid programs of as much structure as possible to allow students' own talents, ingenuity, and interests to guide their development. This approach has produced generations of distinguished scientists and scholars. But it may not work as well for a diverse student body. The ambiguities it allows into the training experience may impose a special burden on students whose identities put their belongingness under suspicion. The open-ended freedom assumed to foster development could leave them in near-constant churn.

It's important to stress that the UC Berkeley College of Chemistry, like GSU, used multiple practices to reduce ambiguity and give support in the setting. Multiple red buttons. Any one practice alone might not be enough. Take procedural justice— the degree to which a community adheres to nondiscriminatory, transparent practices in matters of hiring, promotion, and adjudicating disputes. We humans are exquisitely sensitive to the perception of justice in such matters. Violations break trust and cause churn. But evidence of routine procedural justice may not be enough by itself to secure the trust of people who have been traditionally under stereotype pressure in a setting. It is certainly necessary. But without a multiply evidenced foundation of trust in the setting, no one thing may be sufficient.

5.

The team of researchers who studied Berkeley's College of Chemistry expanded their research. Led this time by Aaron Fisher, a social psychologist in UC Berkeley's Department of Psychology, they surveyed women and underrepresented minorities (URMs) and a random sample of white and Asian males in STEM programs at four universities: UC Berkeley, UCLA, Caltech, and Stanford—499 students in all. They wanted to know, among other things, if there were group differences in the number of publications these students produced, and if so, what caused the difference. The survey also measured possible causes. Their findings reinforced the findings at GSU and Berkeley. White and Asian males did produce more publications—as was the case in most math and physical science departments at UC Berkeley. But this difference was reduced for women and minorities who reported three critical perceptions: that they felt well prepared for graduate school, that they were well received by faculty and fellow students, and that their graduate program was well structured—clear expectations and standards of performance conveyed early on. It's encouraging that the last two of these perceptions are things graduate programs can affect. Faculty can be more receptive. Programs can be better structured to provide consistent communication and support. Simple things that, as illustrated at GSU and Berkeley Chemistry, could meaningfully increase the representation of women and minorities in STEM fields. As Fisher and his group put it: "These findings support the notion that organizational interventions such as clarifying expectations and standards may help reduce academic disparities by potentially alleviating some of the distress associated with graduate education." They go on: "The findings suggest that mitigating factors that negatively affect diversity should not, in principle, require the investment of larger resources." Instead, what was required was "attention to the local culture and structure of individual STEM PhD programs."

6.

In committing to an integrated society, we've committed to a process of inclusion in our institutions, organizations... in the units of our society. A central argument of this book is that these units can be agents of inclusion themselves. GSU and Berkeley Chemistry are two "units" that embody a distinct approach to inclusion. It's an approach made clearer by contrast with more common remediate-to-assimilate approaches—trying to first remediate presumed deficits of the less prepared so they can more easily assimilate into the mainstream of a setting—be it a university, a corporation, a military unit, or a religious order. Though well-intended, and with some successes, remediating to assimilate can wind up stigmatizing the people it's trying to include—the implication being that they lack something, and that they must be remediated before they can fully belong. And perhaps it's the very thing the stereotype alleges about their group. Moreover, as the remediation effort becomes part of the setting, the idea of the group being in need of remediation becomes available to everyone in the setting, often reinforcing stereotypes of the group. Then those being remediated have to worry that their frustration—even when it's no greater than anyone else's—will be taken as confirmation of their deficit. When the setting is important—for example, during transition into college, into the corporate world, into the legal or medical profession—this can be a toxic pressure to live under. It lays down social-psychological conditions that make churn a chronic and alienating experience in the setting.

This book argues instead for a "wise" model of inclusion, as practiced at GSU and Berkeley Chemistry: meeting the students or inductees where they are, with trust in their potential to develop and with a focus on giving them the red buttons—the information, know-how, resources, timely coaching, social capital, and so on—and showing them the way forward, all of which will enable them to stay in the setting and cope well. These things lower ambiguity and churn—as illustrated in Pat Neal's effect on me, and in the effects of GSU and Berkeley Chemistry's institution-level strategies.

I'd like to think GSU and Berkeley Chemistry are expanding

the pedagogy of higher education. They've made it work better for the diverse population that we actually have and that our nation in its noblest moments has committed itself to serve in higher education. They haven't dropped the practice of giving grades, or jettisoned the lecture format, or lessened their commitment to research excellence. They haven't restricted their commitment to a narrow sector of the population. Rather, they've added capacities that detect and meet the developmental needs of all students, including the less resourced and identity-threatened. They don't lean back, presuming to select students who have what it takes to succeed in their institution. They lean in; they take responsibility for *developing* students' abilities and talents. And following this developmental approach, they've built solid foundations of institutional trust that greatly facilitate student success.

I have focused here on higher education—the terrain I know best. But as an approach to inclusion, these developmental strategies could well generalize to K-12 schools, corporations, small businesses, nonprofits, military units, and churches. It's worth noting that the efforts at GSU and Berkeley's College of Chemistry converged on the same two aspects of institutional functioning: the orientation that students got as they entered the institution and the degree to which program requirements inside the institution were well-structured. It's easy to miss the connection between these features of a setting and inclusion. We often assume that socialization to a setting and learning its structure can be left to informal processes—picked up by people on their own or with informal help from others in the setting—or that a light orientation and welcome will do. And of course for the well-acculturated and those not living under identity threat, this may be sufficient. But for the identity-threatened, for all the reasons outlined here, this kind of informality may leave them in an unsettling pool of ambiguity. It's probably no accident that in achieving effective inclusion, both GSU and Berkeley Chemistry converged on the same two aspects of institutional functioning—orientation and program structure. These two areas are where they got the biggest bang for their buck. Could this be an approach to inclusion that generalizes to other large organizations and institutions? Could this approach be part of a broader understanding of how to expand opportunity in our society? Part of an Integration 2.0?

CHAPTER 8

Making Guiding Paradigms Wise

K–12 SCHOOLING AND LOW-INCOME STUDENTS

IN ARISTOTLE'S TIME AND EARLIER, one paradigm people used to understand astronomical phenomena was of the sky as a canopy with tiny holes in it that at night let in light from the "other side." It was an understanding that explained observable things—like twinkling stars. That's how paradigms work; they're an understanding of some aspect of the world that, once in place, shapes what's logical to say or think about that aspect of the world. Once you understand the sky as a canopy, for example, it makes sense to ask, "How high is the sky?"

I discussed in chapter 6 how features of a setting can affect people's ability to trust it—to trust that, despite negative stereotypes about their identity that could apply to them in the setting, they would be safe from those stereotypes in that *particular* setting. But what about the overall paradigm of a setting? What about how the setting sees its purpose, the assumptions it makes about how to fulfill that purpose, and the systems and practices it puts in place to realize that purpose? *Can the paradigm that defines and organizes a setting itself be a source of identity threat to some people, perhaps enough so to affect their trust, comfort, and performance?*

I could explore this question in relation to many areas of society: the paradigms that guide legal education in the United States; how corporations socialize new employees into their organizational culture; how professional athletic teams and military units do the same. But following my own expertise, I will focus again on education, this time on low-income students and K–12 schooling. The question of how to make our K–12 schools more effective for low-income students is of major importance to American society. But I also hope that this exploration will illustrate how the paradigm that guides a setting can have effects of its own, effects that go beyond those of its parts and that can indeed affect the trust critical to its fulfilling its function. I begin with how this question and K–12 schooling came to my attention.

1.

On Thanksgiving eve several years ago, trying to retire early to bed, I made the mistake of turning on *Poor Kids*, a PBS *Frontline* documentary on childhood poverty. The story was about a white family—a single mom with two children, a twelve-year-old son, Tyler, and a ten-year-old daughter, Kaylie—living in a stark farmhouse on the outskirts of Stockton, Iowa, in 2012. At one point the mom totals her monthly income at $1,480 against bills of $1,326 before she'd paid for transportation, clothes, or food. Kaylie explains how if you wait long enough hunger sometimes just passes. Tyler describes how they often swap milk for cereal or cereal for milk but rarely have them together.

DURING THE DAY Kaylie and a friend "canned"—they went around Stockton collecting soda and beer cans to redeem. "I like to go canning to make money. I walk the whole town," Kaylie said. The girls were a team, on an adventure. They poked and snooped and made up stories about what they saw. They eventually filled two plastic garbage bags with cans, put them down beside a community center building, and went off to the adjoining playground. Looking up after a while, they saw Tyler trying to make off with the bags of cans—perhaps out of brotherly teasing, but perhaps out of something more than that. Kaylie and her friend run after him, frantically yelling "drop 'em," "drop 'em." Catching him, Kaylie pulls Tyler's T-shirt while her friend gets the bags out of his hands. The bags drop to the ground. Tyler chuckles cynically in defeat but then in a flash of anger kicks one of the bags right into Kaylie's chest. She stands there, immobilized, outraged, and then stomps off, out of the camera's range. The camera stays with Tyler, who, trying to recover his calm, saunters over to a garbage can and begins rummaging through it. His anger and despair are palpable—his family's painful poverty has cast him into a low-status position in town and in school.

It occurred to me, now completely awake, that the anger and alienation in Tyler's face as he kicked those cans revealed a fundamental challenge for American education and society. It is perhaps our nation's greatest inclusion challenge: how to get kids like Tyler who, under the weight of deprivation and low status, find it hard to *trust* that schooling will serve them well, that it will better connect them to our economy and society. Sixteen to seventeen percent of US children under eighteen live in poverty—that is a family of four (one that includes two children under the age of eighteen) living on less than $30,900 per year.* This statistic goes to 38 percent if you include children who are merely low-income—a family of four living on less than $32,150 per year.

Among our thirty-seven peer nations—the Organization for Economic Cooperation and Development (OECD) nations—only four have a higher percentage of children living in poverty than we do. Since 2013, a slim majority of students in our public schools, 50 to 51 percent, are poor or low-income. Can our schools deal with poverty on this scale? *Do we have the right educational paradigm to reach the Tylers of our society?*

We do have a dominant education paradigm—what is sometimes called the "cognitive-accountability" paradigm. Its foundational principle is that the purpose of education is the transmission of knowledge and cognitive skills, especially those critical to our society and economy. In this framework, educators and schools are held accountable for the results of tests and other indicators that measure that transmission.

---

* According to the US Department of Health and Human Services, whether this dollar figure refers to gross or net income depends upon the federal agency determining if a family is or is not eligible for assistance.

This paradigm intensified its grip in the United States, when, in the early 2000s, our students did badly on the PISA exam. The PISA (Programme for International Student Assessment), first conducted in 2000 and repeated every three years, compares fifteen-year-olds in math, science, and reading across sixty-five countries, including today's thirty-eight OECD nations. In 2012, among the then thirty-four OECD countries, the US ranked twenty-sixth in math and seventeenth in reading. In 2022, we were twenty-seventh in math and sixth in reading among the thirty-eight OECD countries. Our schools get most of the blame, even though poverty itself is a substantial factor, since test score gaps between worse- and better-off students exist before they begin school. No Child Left Behind (NCLB, 2002) was the bipartisan legislation that gave an ensuing era of school reform its legal framework and national scope. The Every Student Succeeds Act (ESSA, 2015) relaxed NCLB's control over the nation's testing program and encouraged states to use non-test-based evaluations, but it retains cognitive tests as a chief source of accountability.

Yet as Thomas Kuhn's *The Structure of Scientific Revolutions* reminds us, paradigms do shift, usually when several things go wrong with the dominant one.

Perhaps the biggest problem with the cognitive-accountability paradigm is that it hasn't worked that well. Test scores (our PISAs, for example) haven't improved much. The test score gap between rich and poor has increased. And the use of tests in accountability has had notorious unintended consequences, ranging from "teaching to the test," especially in low-income schools, to schools cheating to better their test score profiles, and even to teachers leaving the profession.

Moreover, cognitive tests don't predict future achievement any better than the character traits our grandmothers stressed: perseverance, ability to delay gratification, resilience, and so on. The goal of the Perry Preschool Project in Ypsilanti, Michigan, in the 1960s was to help low-income children get the skills they'd need for school and life. The project measured "hard" cognitive skills, assessed by tests, and "softer" character traits like persistence and getting along with others, assessed by teachers and self-reports. Looking at how these children grew up, the Nobel Prize-winning economist James Heckman and his colleagues found that "softer" traits predicted children's life outcomes—whether they finished college, their income level, and the quality of their jobs—better than "harder" cognitive skills measured by tests. Kirabo Jackson, a Northwestern University economist, found essentially the same thing for the entire 2005–2012 cohort of North Carolina ninth graders—573,963 students. Their character—this time measured through behaviors like attendance, on-time graduation, suspensions, and grade point average—predicted life outcomes such as college attendance and later income better than their cognitive test scores.

Still, these two facts—that Grandma's traits predict as well as cognitive tests, and that a national regime of test score accountability didn't improve overall scores or those of poor kids—raises a distinct possibility: that education's cognitive-accountability paradigm itself is flawed in ways that may hurt already disadvantaged students.

MAKING GUIDING PARADIGMS WISE

Think of Tyler showing up to school—possibly prospecting for food in trash cans along the way. He's undoubtably in a preoccupying state of churn. He knows how he might be seen and treated in school based on the poverty and status of his family, on skill and vocabulary deficiencies possibly tied to that poverty, on having a dialect and even clothes that reflect his social status, on not having seen much of the world outside his neighborhood, and so on. He might soon be given a standardized test. From the perspective of cognitive accountability, this would be necessary to slot him into a skill-appropriate curriculum or program to raise his skills. Given his life circumstances, he'd likely not do well and then be assigned, for example, to a lower reading group—an assignment that could unfold into other lower-curriculum assignments over the long run, perhaps indefinitely.

And how would Tyler take this? As a signal that his potential is not highly regarded? What evidence would he have to the contrary? Remember, he's also hungry and probably feels lower-status socially. And these things are on top of the distracting demands that go with being poor—from prospecting for food on the way home to looking after his sister every day. Imagine the content of his churn—the argument in his head about how important school is to him and whether he can *trust* that at some point—given his circumstances—he could have good experiences there. Perhaps he should just disengage a bit. Maybe skateboarding is a place he could have more friends.

What he needs when he gets to school is something other than cognitive accountability—its good intentions notwithstanding. He needs signals that address his churn and that help resolve it: signs from adults and fellow students, for example, that he belongs in that school, that he is valued for who he is and who he can be, and that he is seen as having the potential to succeed there. And it wouldn't hurt if he found some things about school interesting. For example, if his homeroom teacher read the class a compelling story every morning to get the day rolling. He needs signals that despite his status—and his churn to the contrary—he can *trust* the school's beneficence toward him.

Yet in his school—very likely in the grip of cognitive accountability—he isn't likely to have such experiences. Rather (as we shall see), he's likely to get a more basic skills curriculum not much connected to his life, needs, or interests; a rigid disciplinary system; and frequent assessments of his cognitive skills that, from his perspective, may reinforce his image as a poor student—to himself and others. It's hard to imagine this approach encouraging Tyler to care about school, to identify with it in the sense of taking school achievement on as something he holds himself accountable to. Seeing this, as I have, feels a little like seeing excessively harsh parenting in a supermarket. You can understand the parent's frustration, even see good intentions. But what's most apparent is that the parent is following a misguided paradigm, one as unreasonable as asking, "How high is the sky?"

Could such misguidance be a root of the educational inequalities that trouble our society? Could an expanded paradigm—one that also focuses on building students' trust in

MAKING GUIDING PARADIGMS WISE

their schools' ability and willingness to invest in them—make a transformative difference?

To answer these questions—and better understand what schooling needs to do to educate less advantaged students—it's important to consider how poverty affects the schooling experience.

2.

Research over the past thirty or so years reveals a compendium of poverty-driven impediments to school success. Some are indirect effects, mediated through poverty's effect on other things. Poorer children are more likely, for example, to have suffered intrauterine stress, a fragmented family structure, and an authoritarian parenting style that can foster relatively weak self-regulatory skills. They are exposed to a smaller range of vocabulary, are read to less, are taken to fewer non-routine places, and are less likely to have adults talk to them in ways that foster logical thinking and participative skills. They are more likely to experience trauma and ongoing stress. Once in school—society's first good chance to engage them—they're most often segregated into schools with other low-income students, with the least experienced teachers who have the highest turnover rates. And, following the assumptions of the cognitive-accountability paradigm, they are most often assigned an unengaging, basic skills curriculum. Even when they wind up in better-off schools, they are often assigned to academic tracks that recapitulate the disadvantages of lower-income schools.

This is a rocky road of obstacles. And there is increasing

evidence that traversing it leaves disturbing traces: effects on brain and nervous system development that can "become permanent differences in neural structure and function, altering the opportunities of children as they grow into adulthood," write Charles Nelson and Margaret Sheridan in their review of this research.

Poverty also pressures the immediate experience of schooling. Brilliant field studies by the MIT behavioral economist Sendhil Mullainathan and the Princeton cognitive psychologist Eldar Shafir, described in their book *Scarcity*, show that the scarcities of poverty (like those of time) can so focus one's attention on immediate demands that little bandwidth is left for planning, learning about options, doing homework, and building relationships and cultural capital. The urgency of his sister's having to rummage through garbage to find enough cans that his family could have milk and cereal at the same breakfast surely narrows Tyler's bandwidth for school.

And, as has been a theme of this book, even the identity of being poor poses challenges. In school, Tyler can't know if he will be judged and treated in terms of negative stereotypes of the poor. What if he answers a question incorrectly in class? What if his teacher offers critical advice or feedback? Is it intended as help, or is it a reflection of how his teacher sees the poor?

Sustained school achievement requires identifying with one's schooling—seeing its value for one's life and viewing it as a possibility for oneself. For middle-class children, this promise of schooling can be taken for granted most of the time. But for

MAKING GUIDING PARADIGMS WISE

Tyler, school fails to help much with his pressing needs. At the same time, it can make him feel worse about himself. It can be hard for him to trust that schooling is an investment that will pay off. *A big way that poverty undermines schooling is to make it seem irrelevant to one's life.*

Succeeding with children in Tyler's straits, then, will likely require going beyond the cognitive-accountability paradigm, beyond remedies like more hours in school, hiring teachers with MA degrees, evidence-based teaching, and so on. To be sure, these things can help, as would teaching these students the non-cognitive traits shown to facilitate school achievement, things like persistence and the ability to delay gratification for the sake of school achievement. All these efforts should be helpful. But I am raising a further concern: Will any of these things help much if these students don't trust the beneficence of their schooling?

A variation on Walter Mischel's famous 1972 marshmallow study speaks to this question. In the Mischel experiment, children from three to five were given a marshmallow and told that if they waited for a while without eating it, they would get a second marshmallow. The length of time they waited for the second marshmallow was the measure of how much they could delay gratification for a later, larger reward. In a follow-up study conducted by Celeste Kidd, Holly Palmeri, and Richard Aslin at the University of Rochester in 2013, the experimenter preceded the marshmallow choice with another task—a coloring book task—and gave the children a set of used crayons. Then, as the children began coloring, the experimenter said he would go get them a newer, better set of crayons. For half of the children, he did so—a promise kept. For the other half, he returned with crayons no newer than the original ones—a promise not kept. All participants then did the marshmallow test. The children who got newer crayons (a promise kept, signaling that they were in a trustworthy environment) waited longer for a second marshmallow than the children who got the older crayons (a promise not kept, signaling a less trustworthy environment). The ability to delay gratification manifested itself when the environment proved reliable, the experimenter trustworthy, but not when it proved unreliable—when the experimenter couldn't be trusted to follow through on his word. All of the children could delay gratification. They had the capacity. But they did so only when it made sense, only when the experimenter showed he could be trusted.

An implication of this experiment is that for any intervention (cognitive or non-cognitive) to be successful, the schooling context should be trustworthy, a place of low churn where students feel reliably supported. Even the personal traits that we take as critical to school success—persistence, the ability to delay gratification, resilience—are situation-specific. They grow and develop best in low-churn situations that people trust, be that a school or some other setting. As noted, Tyler might already have some of these traits in settings he trusts—a skateboarding group he belongs to, a local heavy metal rock club where he works as an usher, or a late-night basketball league. Yet in an unforthcoming school, he may have none of these traits.

3.

So, the cognitive-accountability paradigm may keep out of view, or at least in dim view, something very important to the academic achievement of students like Tyler—the social-psychological dimension of his school experience, including that tied to his identity. The cognitive-accountability paradigm is essentially identity-blind. It knows that this aspect of a student's experience can affect school achievement—for example, that it can be helpful when student experience is shaped by a middle-class background and less so when it is shaped by a lower-income background. But as a paradigm, it prioritizes the cognitive aspects of schooling. When identity differences in school achievement emerge—as with our well-known group-performance gaps—this paradigm doesn't readily turn to addressing the social-psychological aspects of schooling. More often, assuming such gaps are rooted in cognitive deficits, it doubles down on cognitive remediations and less engaging basic skill curicula—all the while missing the importance of students identifying with their schooling. Yet in recent decades, this orientation has begun to crack a bit. Several areas of practice and research have expanded our understanding of what low-income students need to succeed in school: something in addition to cognitive accountability.

Billy Aydlett, principal of Leataata Floyd Elementary School, in Sacramento, California, in describing his low-income students in a 2013 *New York Times* article by Jennifer Kahn, summarized the basic insight of one such area: "What we discovered was that these kids weren't going to be able to make progress on the academics until they'd gotten help with their social and emotional issues." To render this help, K–12 educators have adopted a host of practices, including morning meetings of students and teachers to share experiences and set the tone for the day; journals kept by both students and teachers to track emotions throughout the day; mindfulness and breathing exercises to relax and encourage self-reflection; and instruction in conflict resolution. These social-emotional learning (SEL) practices sensitize students to their emotional lives and foster the development of traits like self-control, curiosity, resilience, and emotion regulation. But they also give them a sense of being seen and valued for who they are—a sense of being in a place more attuned to their needs and experiences, a schooling environment they can more easily identify with.

According to a 2024 report by the RAND Corporation, 83 percent of K–12 schools in the United States include some form of SEL curriculum. The nature and extent of these efforts vary greatly. They rarely reach the level of integrated and comprehensive programming of whole school reforms. Some efforts dominate the school culture. Others are only a few minutes of calming meditation. Nor are they tied together by any single theory of change, other than a broad recognition among educators that for many students, especially in the wake of the pandemic, attention to their social-emotional and mental health needs is critical to their academic progress. Despite this variability in implementation, meta-analyses of their efforts over hundreds of schools consistently show positive effects on school climate and academic performance—often effects that cognitively oriented interventions would aspire to.

I am proud to be associated with another growing area of research and practice showing the significance of social-psychological experience in schooling, especially for students like Tyler who can experience identity and stereotype threat in school. It shows that even small interventions that lessen this threat can dramatically improve students' engagement in school, persistence, and performance—and lastingly so. In chapter 4 I described an early field experiment in this tradition by Cohen, Purdie Greenaway, Garcia, Apfel, and Master. It showed that when seventh-grade Black students had a chance to affirm a valued image of themselves for their teacher—making it less likely that they'd be seen stereotypically—it quickly improved their grades. Just as important, by launching a recursive process of success leading to further success, this writing exercise set them on a path of higher school achievement that lasted throughout high school, even making them more likely to enroll in college than control students who wrote less affirming paragraphs.

Gregory Walton and Geoffrey Cohen tested the effect of a similar intervention at the college level. They exposed freshman to a persuasive message that presented the social stresses of college life as transient and as something everyone experiences. This message improved Black students' grades over their next three years in college when compared to Black students who didn't get this message. How did it do this? Further analysis showed that it helped Black students see college stress as something not peculiar to their identity. It reduced their identity threat. They could trust their environment more—churn less—and their grades reflected it.

A now large and growing literature shows that multiple ways of reducing identity threat can help students who are facing these threats: interventions that, as just described, help students trust their belonging in the setting, as in the Cohen and Walton research; interventions that help students believe that the abilities critical to succeeding in school are not fixed but can be expanded and grown, as in the research of Carol Dweck, Joshua Aronson, Mary Murphy, and David Yeager; interventions that help students see that the culture and perspectives of people who share their identity are recognized and valued in the setting, as in the research and writings of Gloria Ladson Billings, Dorothy Steele, Jason Okonofua, and Becki Cohn-Vargas; and interventions that enable students to affirm, for themselves and for their teachers, valued images of themselves, as in the research of Geoff Cohen, Valerie Purdie Greenaway, and David Sherman.

It's important to remember that these interventions are

not general enhancers of academic performance. They don't act by directly improving the knowledge base or cognitive skills of students—an effect that might be expected from interventions like longer school days or smaller classes that aim to improve learning in all students. They don't hurt students' performance. But they affect it through a different route of action—more social-psychological than directly learning-oriented. For students facing Tyler-type identity threat, they improve performance less by directly affecting their learning than by reducing the identity threat that can otherwise interfere with their learning. That's their route of action, their shared active ingredient. They do it in different ways. But they all change the socio-psychological experience of school for these students. And throughout the now extensive literature testing these effects, it is for these students that these interventions have their largest, most reliable effects.

Looked at from the standpoint of cognitive accountability, these strategies—socio-emotional learning strategies or strategies reducing the identity threat many students can experience in school—can seem beside the point, of marginal importance, not rooted in cognitive principles of learning. But looked at from the standpoint of building students' trust in their schooling and their identification with it, they have a clear unity: They all address Tyler's primary need to trust, care about, and engage with school. The good news here is that from an expanded paradigm—the identification paradigm—falls a much-expanded set of fixes.

4.

Against this emerging picture of what works, one might ask: What do our schools actually do for students, including our Tylers?

In 2007, a research team headed by Robert Pianta, of the University of Virginia School of Education, observed what teachers did in 737 fifth-grade classrooms (87 percent of them in public schools) across 302 school districts over 33 states. The quality of instruction and emotional climate in these classrooms varied considerably, but one thing didn't: 91 percent of every day was dominated by basic skills teaching, largely lectures and whole-class worksheets, replicating a similar pattern of findings by the same researchers for first- and third-grade classrooms The average fifth grader spent 500 percent more time on basic skills instruction than on problem-solving or reasoning activities. And this pattern was especially true in low-income classrooms: 91 percent of those classrooms were rated low in instructional quality and 76 percent were rated low in emotional climate.

Research following the original Pianta report shows that interventions aimed at expanding teachers' instructional focus and skills (some developed by the Pianta team) or that integrate SEL practices into instruction can have positive effects on student outcomes. Yet this research—often using the Classroom Assessment Scoring System (CLASS), developed by the Pianta team—continues to show a dominant focus of K–12 instruction on foundational skills, especially in reading and math, and especially so for low-income and minority students. For example, the above 2024 RAND Corporation survey sampled 3,897 English Language Arts (ELA) teachers and found that foundational reading skills are still at the center of their teaching across all grade levels.

Remember, 50 to 51 percent of our nation's public school students are low-income. Extrapolating from the Pianta research, when they get to school, they are the least likely to get higher-quality instruction or to find themselves in a positive emotional climate. We can safely say, then, that they don't get much of what they need to trust and identify with school. They don't get what they need to lower their churn there and then to elevate our nation's PISA scores, or improve the skills of our workforce, or bring US upward mobility in line with that of many European nations.

How'd we get here?

"The role of education in . . . the integration of new workers into the wage labor system came to dominate the potential role of schooling as the great equalizer and the instrument of full human development," wrote Samuel Bowles and Herbert Gintis in 1976, in their classic *Schooling in Capitalist America*. Under the press of a modernizing economy, we adopted a pragmatic, cognitive-accountability paradigm for education: Any developmental focus on the whole child—as in the pedagogy of the great early twentieth-century reformer John Dewey—had to function within the constraints of this larger accountability.

The kind of schooling that Pianta and his colleagues document is likely a legacy of this pragmatism.

Another such legacy is a bias in what we think students like

Tyler need from school. We stress their cognitive deficits. We see remedies focused on those deficits as most important. We can lose sight of the things, larger and small, that a school can do to first build students' trust in their schooling. In *Improbable Scholars*, David Kirp offers an example of how effective this approach can be, even when scaled up to an entire school district. His focus is on low-income Union City, New Jersey, schools where students score as well as their much better-off suburban counterparts in writing, reading, and math. No silver bullets. No off-the-shelf reform package. Rather, it's stable leadership and day-to-day, year-in, year-out commitment to doing all the big and little things that put expert-tutor wiseness into students' daily lives: child-centered over staff-centered priorities, big investments in preschool, rigorous and integrated curricula, explicit and constant attention to building cultures of respect and confidence in students' potential. The academic mission of these schools is unconditional. But they understand that when a focus on building trust is persistently applied—in curriculum decisions, disciplinary policies, rules for composing student study groups, after-school options, the examples used in presenting STEM material, the hiring of teachers and staff—it can take a school to a tipping point of effectiveness for all students.

This is how good schools—like good restaurants, as my colleague Joshua Aronson pointed out to me—get built. Guiding principles are minutely and persistently applied. We keep track of how they work, and we refine them to better and better effect. It is the ground game of school improvement.

Just how much can be accomplished this way? How big is

MAKING GUIDING PARADIGMS WISE

the claim here? Pretty big, I'd say. The focus, patience, discipline, and persistence needed for school reform in the complex policy and funding world in which most public schools exist today cannot be minimized. School reform is tough. And sustained school reform is . . . a true feat.

That said, I have two reasons for "pretty big" optimism. The first is that the mal-effects of the cognitive-accountability paradigm—which for students like Tyler can be deeply alienating—are relatively correctable. Simply pulling back on the testing regime that is at the heart of the paradigm might substantially improve the academic experience and outcomes of students. It has already happened in many high-performing independent schools and in some of the world's best school systems—famously in Finland, for example.

It's an insight that is spreading. ESSA has given school systems more flexibility in the measures they use to evaluate school performance, reducing the pressure for standardized testing. Many states in recent years have dropped their requirement of standardized high school exit exams. North Carolina's legislature passed a Testing Reduction Act (2019) to reduce the overuse of testing. Similar movements are afoot in Pennsylvania, Texas, and California. A "More Teaching Less Testing" bill was introduced in Congress in 2023 to relax some of the ESSA testing requirements. And as mentioned earlier, many school districts are exploring ways of evaluating student progress that allow more focus on whole-child development—changes that may indeed change what students like Tyler, Kaylie, or a young George Floyd experience as they enter school.

My second reason for optimism is that shifting from a cognitive-accountability paradigm to an identification paradigm—which, as in the Union City schools, sees building students' trust in and identification with school as a priority—can make a major difference. This paradigm is rooted in tactics already shown to have constructive effects on outcomes, especially for low-income students. Research increasingly shows that even small efforts to help students churn less about their belonging and promise in our classrooms—despite their empty stomachs, deficits, ongoing stresses, and negative images of their identity—can have transformative effects. These practices have been used in marginal and scattered ways. The identification paradigm establishes them as a priority in all aspects of schooling.

I will close this chapter with a study that illustrates what this looks like.

THE SOCIAL PSYCHOLOGISTS Jason Okonofua, David Paunesku, and Gregory Walton asked thirty-one math teachers from five low-income, largely minority California middle schools to complete two brief online modules designed to evoke an empathic mindset—specifically that student misbehavior can stem from developmental challenges and social pressures as much as from deeper problems. They further prompted them with the sentence: "A teacher who makes his or her students feel heard, valued, and respected shows them that school is fair and they can grow and succeed there." Over the next year,

MAKING GUIDING PARADIGMS WISE

teachers who got the empathy prompt suspended only half the number of students who were suspended by a control group of teachers who did not get the prompt. This happened despite K-12 suspensions having increased nationally from 1.7 million to anywhere from 3.2 to 5 million from 1974 to 2011-2012 (a disproportionate percentage of those suspended were minority and low-income students). No policy change, no training program, no teacher accountability system, just a prompt, a nudge to empathize with student experience.

CHAPTER 9

Going Forward

A PERSPECTIVE AND A STRATEGY

1.

I have tried to define churn and identify principles of wiseness that can combat it. But a broader question remains: Is there a general approach to achieving wiseness in the settings we live and work in—even as the people in the settings churn vigorously about their group interests and vulnerabilities and the histories of injustice that lie between them?

As noted, in the early days of the civil rights movement, the ideal of a redemptive "beloved community" served this purpose. It stressed our shared humanity. It invited people to live the integrated life they were fighting for in American society. Its appeal was rooted in the redemptive Judeo-Christian ethic that guided Martin Luther King Jr., John Lewis, and others in highlighting the inhumanity of segregation. It inspired resistance to segregation, sometimes at the cost of people's lives. Yet the idea of "beloved community" feels anachronistic, rooted as it was in a time of shared religiosity that gave the ideal a galvanizing power it would lack today.

In its place, *Churn* proposes a strategy of trust-building—predicated on the assumption that we trust those, independent of their identity, who help us function well in a setting.

An important step in this strategy is perspective-taking—in particular, trying to see settings and people in them less as an observer and more as an actor, more as people behaving in the setting would see things. The observer's and actor's perspectives can lead to very different understandings of the same behavior.

An example comes from my own research on stereotype threat. In trying to understand how negative stereotypes affect people, the dominant perspective of twentieth-century social science has been that of an observer. To an observer, it's the stereotyped people themselves who are the salient part of the phenomenon. It's easy to think, then, that the primary effects of a stereotype are on the people who are its target, that it somehow changes them. An argument follows: that regular exposure to the stereotype—having it "hammered, hammered, hammered" in, as the famous personality psychologist Gordon Allport put it—causes people to eventually "internalize" it. That is, believe it. This in turn causes psychic damage or low self-esteem that contributes to poorer economic, educational, and health outcomes for the group.

All quite plausible from an observer's perspective. In fact, it's a view expressed by no less than W. E. B. Du Bois, Sigmund Freud, and Gordon Allport in relation to Blacks, Jews, and women. And of course it dominates our commonsense psychology about how stereotypes affect people.

The actor's perspective is different. The actor—the person in the setting coping with, among other things, the possibility of being stereotyped—is not looking at himself. He's looking out at the circumstances he's dealing with. It's those circumstances that stand out to him, not himself. He's likely, then, at least in large part, to see the effects of stereotypes differently than an observer: not as an idea about his group that he comes to believe at the expense of his own confidence and life outcomes but more simply as a threat posed by other people in the setting. He sees their stereotype-driven judgments and treatment of him that could disadvantage him in important settings like school, a business situation, or a traffic stop.

So, to the question of how to build trust in diverse settings, *Churn* recommends taking the actor's perspective. It's a mindset that searches for what people in the setting are contending with, including what they are contending with because of their identities. And it is precisely this search that the observer's perspective, and its ally, color-blindness, discourage us from taking. This can require effort, even education. But it brings to the fore information, experiences, and ideas missed by an observer's perspective.

2.

Being lower-income than most other students in his high school, college, and graduate school, Tim Renick easily identified with Georgia State's lower-income student body—students who often held outside jobs, sometimes more than one, to support themselves and their families. So when thinking through problems in his eventual role as Georgia State's vice provost for enrollment, registration, and financial aid, he found it easy to take the actor's perspective, the perspective of his students. One of his early challenges in this role, as described in Andrew Gumbel's *Won't Lose This Dream*, was a glitch in Georgia's HOPE Scholarship program for low-income students. This program gives as much as four years of support for tuition, books, and fees to any resident attending a public or private postsecondary institution in Georgia—if they maintain a minimum 3.0 grade point average (GPA). But if they miss this standard by even a tenth of a grade point, they lose their scholarship. Reflecting the stress of this loss, students who lose their scholarship are then only half as likely to graduate as students who never had a HOPE scholarship in the first place.

An observer might see this as due to something about the students involved. After all, the state had given them a considerable hand up. For them to not graduate, then, must mean that they lacked gumption, motivation, self-esteem, resilience. Renick saw things differently. Taking the students' perspective, he looked less at student characteristics and more at their life circumstances—things he could help with. He devised a Georgia State amendment to the HOPE Scholarship. If a student's GPA fell to 2.75—a level that would normally cause the student to lose the scholarship—he got Georgia State's private foundation to give them a second chance: $1,000, to be used over the next two semesters so they could stay in school and bring their GPA back up to 3.0 to regain their scholarship. He called it Keep HOPE Alive (KHA). It didn't work. Only 9 percent of the students who got KHA support were able to resume their scholarships.

An observer might have said, "I told you so." But Renick still stuck with the actor's perspective. He investigated the students' experience. He found something troubling. Losing the scholarship meant that they then had to pay their own tuition—a substantial increase in their expenses even with the $1,000 from KHA. To pay, they often charged tuition to credit cards. Then, to avoid defaulting on those cards, they often left school for further employment, never to return. His surmise: Perhaps they didn't know how to deal with the onslaught of pressures that befell them when they lost their scholarship—increased tuition costs, increased credit card debt (or default), on top of intense pressure to regain a 3.0 GPA within two semesters. His solution: helping them cope with the financial and psychological stresses that come with losing their scholarships. He required students getting KHA funds to also take training—provided by Georgia State—in financial literacy and the academic organizational skills that Pat Neal helped me with. With these requirements in place, the percentage of students who regained their scholarships after having lost them went from 9 percent to 60 percent.

3.

You can probably tell I like the actor's perspective. Yet taking it can be difficult. We must somehow get into the actor's shoes, see the situation as they see it. That can take effort, sometimes even research, certainly patience and openness to hearing how others experience a situation. Look at the patience and effort Renick put into understanding how students experienced the loss of their HOPE Scholarships. He leaned in. He talked to those who'd lost their scholarships. He talked to colleagues and collaborators. He developed a sophistication in using data and data analysis techniques to learn students' needs. His and his colleagues' success attests to the value of this effort, especially in a diverse setting.

The actor's perspective has its critics. Several come easily to mind: that it can be "excusiology"—using "circumstances" to excuse people from taking responsibility for their own outcomes in life. It can be seen as treating people with "soft expectations" that stagnate their development; as a guise for liberal ideology. It can be said to foster helicopter and snowplowing behavior in parents who try to remove every obstacle from the path of their "snowflake" children. And so on. Of course, some of the criticism has merit. Each of us at one time or another has seen the downside of too much support when people should have been pressed to take more responsibility for themselves. Overuse of the actor's perspective can be as damaging as overuse of the observer's perspective.

But when it's overused, it's usually because the people using it haven't done their homework. They haven't leaned in and gotten on the ground in the setting to learn what actors are actually experiencing there. They are relying instead on preconceptions or even ideological depictions of what the actors are experiencing. And generally, such lack of effort doesn't go unnoticed by people in the setting. It can undermine intergroup trust. Whereas the presence of this effort, à la Renick, signals wiseness and reinforces trust—enough to weaken the Tajfelian tendency for identities to mistrust each other.

4.

Can this approach be formed into a usable strategy for building foundational trust and lowering churn in diverse settings? I believe so, and propose a strategy with three goals: seeing, welcoming, and supporting.

Seeing. Robert Moses—a leader of the Student Nonviolent Coordinating Committee (SNCC), Harlem-born, a graduate of Hamilton College—took on as his first SNCC assignment the organizing of a voter registration drive in Jackson, Mississippi. It would eventually spur the passage of the 1965 Voting Rights Act. Moses believed that immersion in the local community was the first step in organizing it to take on an ambitious challenge. The aim, he believed, was to participate, to connect with people, to listen patiently—attending to particulars of their experience, to what caused what, what the community believed its needs were, which solutions might work best and inspire others. He paid attention to what people did as much as to what they said and thereby learned which individuals could be relied upon to lead. And only then did SNCC staff join in the development of strategies for change. Like Renick at Georgia State, Moses in Mississippi was *seeing*. He put it simply: "If you really want to do something with somebody else, really want to work with that person, the first thing you have to do is make a personal connection. You have to find out who it is you are working with."

I think of *seeing* as the most important component of trust-building. To better understand it, let's consider how easy it is not to see—for example, what a more conventional approach to fixing Georgia State's dropout problem might have been. A committee would have been formed. I've served on several and appointed others. The committee members are not actors in the situation—they're not students, for the most part. They're observers. What's foremost in their thinking is the dropout problem itself, and the students who are dropping out. This channels the committee's focus. What is it about these students that leads them to drop out—poor academic preparation, too much social media, the increasing prevalence of mental health issues on campus, generational issues?

Given the committee's focus, these ideas make sense—they can even seem obvious. Remedies are proposed and some are implemented—academic remediation and tutoring programs, hiring more academic advisors, strengthening mental health services, and so on. (Social media regulation . . . not so much.) Sometimes, given the committee's mission, these programs are targeted more at groups with bigger dropout problems—say, low-income or minority students. Sometimes financial aid is involved. And these efforts may indeed produce modest gains. But in my experience, they're rarely transformative. I've never seen this kind of effort move a university's six-year graduation rate from 32 percent to 54 percent in eleven years, as happened at Georgia State from 2003 to 2014.

The difference between this conventional approach and what happened at Georgia State, I would suggest again, is that Renick, like Robert Moses, was *seeing*. He wasn't a student. He wasn't an actor. But he was immersed in the university in a way that brought him close to student experience. He taught there for decades before becoming a vice provost. He'd been a highly successful teacher and mentor. He'd seen student frustration caused by a lack of social capital and financial resources and by troubles with university bureaucracy. Also, he wasn't thinking just about the dropout problem. He was thinking—more like students themselves would think—about the larger question of what enables a person to stay in college. He could see that with early detection and timely advising, students could often overcome "deficits" in preparation that would otherwise have seemed insurmountable. He could see that students benefited from being part of smaller networks. He could see that all students had these challenges to some degree, and that targeting programs at specific groups could stigmatize those groups and alienate other students. He could see that it was better to develop supports for all students, even though some groups might use them more than others. He could see that this would allow student supports to become normative, not stigmatizing, in the university community. He could see that students needed financial aid when their families suffered unexpected financial shocks. And all the while, he was doing—implicitly and explicitly—the kind of "cues audit" developed by Mary Murphy and her colleagues described in chapter 6, to understand how the university context affected students' comfort and morale. Renick's *seeing* led to a different understanding of student success at Georgia State and gave its students more of what they needed to stay in college. And like trusting someone who helps you prepare for a Chicago winter, students could come to trust Georgia State. They could settle in, feel more secure, churn less, have a better college experience. And, by the way, drop out less—a lot less—transforming an entire university.

Seeing as a conscious step in building trust has another advantage: It can help identify the trust-building tactic that is best suited to a setting. In Renick's case, *seeing* pointed to a lack of resources and the absence of skills needed to manage that lack. In another setting, the threat to trust may not involve resources. It may stem more from a climate of identity threat—a manager's language that persistently conveys an identity-status hierarchy, or people facing particular forms of stereotype in a setting, such as women in an advanced graduate physics seminar, or white males in an intense diversity workshop. Under these circumstances a social-psychological intervention may be sufficient.

The larger point is that the effort to foster trust in diverse settings—a university, a small business, a sixth-grade classroom, a new start-up, a medical office, a magazine—is likely to be incomplete without *seeing*, without, as much as possible, walking in the shoes of the people involved.

Welcoming. When we enter a setting that is important to us—a university, a recreational area, a diversity workshop, a workplace—a churn-causing question hangs in the air: How will my identity—who I am—affect my experience here? To build trust in diverse settings, it's important to give people a welcoming experience that addresses that question.

Yet as shown in the Stephens research described in chapter 6, welcomes can go wrong: they can alienate people, even if inadvertently, as well as welcome them. Recall the finding: When a welcome letter ostensibly written by a college president emphasized independence, finding one's own passion, and working independently, working-class students were affected enough that they performed worse than non-working-class students on a subsequent verbal reasoning test. And at orientation, when independence was emphasized but no mention was made of communitarian values, working-class students got lower grades than other students on a subsequent test. These were students whose admission credentials and high school grades were on par with those of everyone else participating in the experiment. There's a lesson in these findings: When bringing a diversity of people into a setting, it's especially important that welcoming be inclusive. When it's not—again, even inadvertently so—it can have serious consequences.

Yet this fact isn't always obvious. Organizations can see welcoming as the first step in socializing new members into the culture of the organization. It's to this motivation that the Stephens findings suggest caution. It is important not to be so focused on socialization as to risk alienating some of the people the effort is trying to welcome. There is a need for balance in welcoming. While not diminishing a setting's defining function and values, it's important to stress that different perspectives, interests, skills, and insights can be of value in the setting. It's difficult to feel welcome if acceptance is seen as conditional on affiliating with values one is just becoming aware of.

Greyston Bakery, in Yonkers, New York, is the primary supplier of brownies to Ben & Jerry's ice cream company and has its own line of baked goods sold at Whole Foods. It's also committed to serving its low-income surrounding neighborhood—an effort that begins with the way it welcomes potential employees. It uses an Open Hiring model that explicitly welcomes "those who face rejection elsewhere." It replaces "scrutiny with trust." It does away with background checks, résumés, drug testing, credit checks, and interviews. People are hired first come, first served. Once hired, they serve a six-month apprenticeship at slightly above minimum wage before being offered a long-term job. The wiseness of a welcome like this for this population of potential employees—some of whom have criminal records—can't be overlooked. For this population, the question of whether their identity would bar them from belonging in a strong company like Greyston would be a burning question. The genius of Greyston is to have devised an enthusiastic, open-eyed welcoming system that, while serving the company's needs, puts this burning question to rest—enabling the transformation of countless lives over the years. About 40 percent of its apprentices make it to full employment and join Local 53, which is part of the Bakery, Confectionery, Tobacco Workers and Grain Millers International Union—an impressive number, considering the poverty-related stresses in this community. Greyston has done all of this while remaining a profitable company in a distressed community.

Not all organizations can do what Greyston does. Their practices are an adaptation to their circumstances. Greyston illustrates one way of implementing a broadly useful understanding: For inclusion in a diverse organization to work, people must feel, at the outset, that they can be valued, can contribute, and can in some way succeed. With this achieved, Greyston demonstrates that the people involved, and the organization, can thrive.

Supporting. After welcoming comes support: giving people the know-how to manage the challenges and the opportunities inherent in a setting and, as much as possible, related challenges in their lives. This is important. It helps put to rest the nagging question that spurs churn, the question about whether your identity will disadvantage you. It doesn't rule out the possibility. But it diminishes its likelihood. It changes the feel of even larger organizations. I point again to the examples of Georgia State and UC Berkeley Chemistry. More than assertions about institutional fairness, commitment to equity, and so on, these schools built trust by actually giving students the help they needed.

And from these examples, several guidelines for support follow.

    a.) Help should be less about getting outcomes and more about supplying the knowledge and know-how needed by people in the setting to achieve those outcomes. In biblical terms, help should be less about giving them fish than about teaching them how to fish. Too much focus on outcomes can worsen people's churn. It raises questions about their belonging. But mainly it leaves them with fewer skills to sustain success.

    b.) To the extent possible, it's good for this help to be made available to everyone in the setting—as at Georgia State and UC Berkeley Chemistry. Offering help to just some groups—as we've learned from decades of trying this through various forms of remediation—can wind up stigmatizing those groups and worsening the stereotype threat and churn they experience.

    c.) Help is less about exhorting people to take on goals or embody strengths of character (in the form of ambition, resilience, open-mindedness) and more about how to do specific things that enable them to make progress in a setting. Progress is less a follow-on to exhortations about taking on challenges than taking on challenges is a follow-on to the confidence that progress gives us.

d.) Relatedly, it's probably wise, especially at the outset of a support effort, to focus people on small, manageable goals that lead incrementally to larger achievements. A focus on large goals can drive us into churn before we get started. Considerable evidence suggests that such efforts are also facilitated by a growth mindset. This idea, as we have seen, is that understanding our abilities as expandable and capable of growing, rather than as given and fixed, can lower churn and motivate the development of persistence and resilience—and ultimately achievement.

e.) As a last principle, an ounce of early intervention is probably worth a pound of remediation—maybe two pounds. The sooner people get the knowledge and know-how needed in a setting, the greater impact that knowledge and know-how can have, and the more they will trust the setting as a place where their needs will be met. Being able to detect when students need help early in their STEM coursework enabled GSU's advising, counseling, and tutoring systems to have a major impact on students' persistence in these fields—not unlike the effect of the early orientation program at UC Berkeley's College of Chemistry.

5.

A distinction between strategy and tactics is useful here. Strategy tells us how to go about doing something. Seeing, welcoming, and supporting are parts of a strategy for building trust and reducing churn in diverse settings. But they don't tell us exactly what to do. That's what tactics are—the specific things that implement the strategy in specific settings. Typically, for any strategic goal there are multiple tactical options. To *see*, for example, one might partner with informants from the setting who know it well, or move into the setting as an ethnographer, or rely on one's own long-term experience in the setting, or use records and archival data to better understand how the setting works, or all the above. To welcome, one might design a three-week orientation before the school year begins, like that of Berkeley Chemistry; or one might organize small, rotating get-to-know-each-other sessions where people have an opportunity to share enough about themselves that stereotypes begin to fade from use. To support, one might develop a chatbot that answers questions at any time—day or night, like the one Georgia State has—or one might assign mentors to new employees, with regular meetings structured in.

In my experience, there is something important to understand about tactics: Their effectiveness is often situationally specific. A given tactic may work well in one setting, inspiring hope. But then not work at all in a different setting, or even backfire. Yet when this happens, it may not be the fault of the tactic. It may be a problem of its fit in the setting. A college welcome letter that inspires students in an upper-middle-class high school may alienate students in a working-class high school. Diversity training may work well in a setting that has built a strong culture of trust but backfire in a setting of new or transient employees. Mismatches of tactics to settings can happen. This is why *seeing* is so important. It develops understandings of a setting that help avoid mismatches. It is important, then, to caution against faith in tactics as silver bullets—generally effective across multiple settings.

Successful efforts at building trust are often achieved through trial-and-error experimentation in the local setting in which they are to be used. Remember how Renick handled the problem of students losing their Hope Scholarships. He started small. He tried things and kept track of their effect, jettisoning or improving what didn't work, incrementally expanding what did work, until he and his colleagues had essentially transformed a university. That's what I mean by trial-and-error experimentation—modifying systems to better meet, in that case, student needs. A strategy like seeing, welcoming, and supporting can guide the search for tactics needed to build trust. But the process isn't complete without the further effort of developing tactics to implement the strategy, often through trial and error.

6.

A classic early experiment by the pioneering social psychologist Melvin Lerner and his colleague Carolyn Simmons asked an important question: How do people respond to the perception of injustice? To find out, Lerner and Simmons brought small groups of subjects into the laboratory, ostensibly to help researchers understand how people react to seeing signs of pain in others. Through a one-way mirror, subjects saw a woman they believed was receiving an electric shock every time she made a mistake on a learning task. They could see the victim but assumed she could not see them. (She was an actress who received no electric shocks but acted as if she did.) The question of the experiment was how people would rate the personality and character of this victim.

Lerner argued as follows: To feel comfortable in the world, we need to believe the world is basically just—that generally people get what they deserve. Thus when we see a person suffering for little reason, it upsets us by implying that maybe the world isn't just. And to restore that injured image, we might actually derogate such a victim—blame them for their suffering—as a way of restoring our needed belief that the world is just, and that people do in fact get what they deserve.

In one of the more surprising findings in the history of social psychology, this is just what happened. Subjects derogated the victim, downgrading her personality and character.

But the experiment included another condition—subjects had a chance to help the victim before rating her. Specifically, they could stop the shocks by saying they'd seen enough to make their judgments without further shocks. Interestingly, when subjects could help the victim in this way, they didn't derogate her. They rated her much higher than did subjects who couldn't help her. Why? It seems they could see themselves as agents of justice. They could assume the world was made just by people's actions, and that their helping the victim was an example of that justice. They didn't need to blame the victim in order to retain their faith in a just world. Their own actions manifested that justice.

Seeing, welcoming, and *supporting* can do for us what being able to save the shock victim did for subjects in the Lerner and Simmons experiment. They give us a way of maintaining a sense of justice in the world by making us agents of that justice—not by "canceling" others, but by helping people trust and flourish in the settings in which we live and work. They can yield a peace of mind—low churn, and a sense of connection in the face of difference—that affirms the world's capacity to be, when we lean in to it, a more just place.

CODA

And Everyone Can Do It

1.

It takes only a small difference between groups to put them at odds with each other—remember the boys in the Tajfel experiment downgrading each other after being randomly assigned to meaninglessly different groups. So it isn't surprising that we have so many isms—sexism, racism, anti-Semitism, ableism, tribalism—or that we have anti-white bias and xenophobia, and that they all still have force in our lives.

Churn is about life under the threat of these isms. Research by social psychologists like John Dovidio, Jennifer Eberhardt, James Jones, Patricia Devine, Samuel Gaertner, Thomas Pettigrew, Tom Tyler, Susan Fiske, Gordon Allport, and others has revealed a lot about where the isms come from, how they function and operate, and how to reduce their impact. Generally, things that make it easier for us to see each other's shared humanity reduce the isms and their impact. For example, sharing a superordinate identity can allow people with normally conflicted sub-identities to get on better—as when Democrats and Republicans face a national security threat, reminding them that we're all Americans. Or desegregation itself—merely bringing people of different identities into contact with each other can often reduce prejudice between them, especially when they are of equal status. Countless educational interventions aim to reduce prejudice—interventions that make us aware of our capacity for bias, that give us prejudice-reducing information about other groups, that teach us how to avoid prejudices. Recall the example mentioned earlier of teaching symphony orchestras to audition musicians hidden by screens to avoid gender and racial bias.

To these efforts, *Churn* adds another focus: building trust in diverse settings, trust that reduces the churn that puts tension between us, that can keep us apart, and that can itself spawn prejudicial beliefs.

We are in an era of restricted options for addressing issues related to inclusion and equality. As I noted at the outset, I am saddened by this. Can we as a society really make progress toward equality without these efforts, or improved versions of them? I doubt it. I see *Churn*'s trust-building strategies as an additional way forward, not as a substitute for other efforts.

Churn has focused on building trust in the organizational units of society—schools, classrooms, medical offices, small businesses, academic departments, science and engineering laboratory groups. These are places where seeing, welcoming, and supporting can become operational and normative.

AND EVERYONE CAN DO IT

Yes, these settings can often be steeped in bureaucracy and tradition, even grand tradition. They can seem impossible to change—even when they are smaller and ostensibly more manageable. But think of the incrementalism illustrated in the College of Chemistry at UC Berkeley. It was being pragmatic when it found its way to practices that illustrate seeing, welcoming, and supporting. Seeing was clearly central. Faculty and staff kept a close eye on what students needed. Georgia State used data analytics to do the same thing. In both cases, it wasn't the availability of new pedagogy, or consultants' advice, or even a special desire to diversify their programs that produced their success. It was a decision not to accept medium results. It was in that pursuit that these strategies proved useful—helping to transform lower-trust environments into higher-trust, lower-churn communities.

Against this ancient problem, *Churn* is looking for additional traction. Despite our identity differences, despite the histories and resentments tied to them that can get between us, despite the prejudices and cultural differences that can further get between us, *Churn* affirms that our shared humanity can be a basis of community. It affirms that retreating to our tribes like the Tajfel boys, while valuable under important circumstances, is not so inevitable as to keep us from forming community.

2.

The last few chapters focused on how to design institutions and the paradigms that shape them—how to form wise communities. In closing, I return to the question of how we as individuals can help organizations and relationships be higher-trust and lower-churn. For example, how should the parents and teacher in the opening vignette of this book behave to achieve a low-churn parent-teacher conference? Many of the characters in this book show what acting with wiseness looks like—Gil Evans, Miles Davis, Tim Renick, Robert Moses, and others. Still, it's clarifying to consider how the parents and teacher in that vignette, despite their role and identity differences, might use *seeing, welcoming,* and *supporting* to build the trust they need to guide the student in question, as well as other students.

It's essential that both parties take a trust-building mindset. If one party drops this commitment, it kills the possibility for the other. Still, as described in chapter 5, to the most situationally empowered falls the responsibility of being a first mover in trust-building. For trust to build in a setting, it must be clear that the more powerfully situated are invested in it. It is they who will have the authority to make organizational room for a trust-building connection.

In *seeing*, each party must accept the importance of making a personal connection with the other—must understand, as Robert Moses did in Mississippi, that they should go talk to each other. They should get a sense of what the others are like; how they see their roles (as teacher or parents, for example); what their intentions, hopes, and concerns are; what conditions and circumstances they are contending with; what their needs are. This getting-to-know-you effort is worth a lot. It conveys respect. And it helps the parties understand each other's needs—for example, in the parent-teacher conference itself, and in going forward as teacher and mentors. It tells each party what would be helpful to the others and it gives both parties some assurance that they are reasonably well understood.

The resulting connection shapes the interpretation of what follows. It helps people disambiguate their experience in the direction of trust. Should the teacher have to convey concern about some aspect of the student's development, a connection helps the parents trust it.

The time spent *seeing* each other and each other's circumstances, prior to the conference or at its beginning, should pay off in trust-building. It could be seen as superfluous, as something that shouldn't be expected of either party. But in fact, especially considering identity and role differences, it is likely essential to their developing trust.

Welcoming, in the context of the parent-teacher conference, means welcoming the perspectives of the other party. The temptation, of course, is to view the conference as a chance to express one's own views. And it is. That's its purpose, in part. But for trust to build, each party has to feel that the other welcomes their views, even when they may not agree with them. When that door shuts, mistrust and churn take over.

Perhaps the best way to do this is to be curious. Welcoming is an invitation to hear, with interest, the other party's experience and thinking. Tactically, this means asking questions more—questions that help supplant defensiveness with curiosity—and explaining oneself less.

As the parents and teacher get to know each other, *supporting* means helping each other realize their goals. The teacher might set up a rhythm of communication with the parents. She might brief them on how they can augment what she is doing in the classroom. And the parents, based on what they can do, and on what the teacher and school need, can seek ways to be helpful—from chaperoning field trips to bringing in materials that help the teacher implement her plans. As trust builds in the relationship, it can deepen mutual understanding. This is important. Few things are as trust-building as real help. And few things frustrate trust-building as much as parties withholding help or not recognizing each other's needs.

As the parents and teacher recognize a shared commitment to students, as trust between them grows, churn fades. The identity difference between them becomes, if not insignificant, then not unsurmountable either. In fact, with trust, that difference can become an enriching resource for both parties. The American experiment can work.

Like many Americans, I would like to believe it could work without any particular attunement to trust-building. But in light of our history as a society, and the fact that identity still shapes our lives, this doesn't strike me as a mature hope. Rather, this book's hope is that the settings of our lives and the people in them can become agents in building that trust. The strategies it offers for doing this carry a clear message. The

AND EVERYONE CAN DO IT

work of building trust doesn't depend on having a particular identity, on being knowledgeable of the trends in identity vocabulary, on being good at signaling their inclusive beliefs, and so on. Its message, as noted, is that trust-building is a game played largely on the ground. It's who listens, listens again, is genuinely welcoming, and collaboratively gives people the help they need to succeed in a setting. It's who's wise. This is the heart of the matter. And anybody—that is, everybody—can do it.

ACKNOWLEDGMENTS

No one writes a book alone. This one is no exception. It arises from a near and far community of people long concerned with the issues addressed in *Churn*. While exempting them from responsibility for errors, biases, or anachronistic or naive ideas that readers may encounter here, I owe a great debt to that community. Within it are friends and former students who are now distinguished faculty and researchers and whose knowledge and wisdom in these areas often far surpass my own. These would include people like Geoff Cohen, Mary Murphy, Valerie Purdie-Greenaway, Greg Walton, Steve Spencer, Joshua Aronson, David Sherman, Valerie Jones Taylor, Kiara Sanchez, Jason Okonofua, and Becki Cohn-Vargus—some of whom have written their own superb books in this area. I think of them as pioneers who have demonstrated the value of taking a social-psychological perspective toward some of society's most tenacious challenges in education, corporate life, and intergroup relations more generally. They've done and continue to do the hard theoretical and empirical work that gives us an expanded understanding of these challenges and what it takes to address them.

This community also includes long-standing and recent colleagues whose depth of knowledge I have long benefited from.

ACKNOWLEDGMENTS

These are close partners-in-crime friends and colleagues like Hazel Markus, Carol Dweck, Ewart Thomas, Richard Nisbett, Brian Lowery, Sean Reardon, Larry Bobo, Henry Louis Gates Jr., and Marcy Morgan and newer colleagues like Jordan Starck and Steven Roberts. My colleagues have simply been one of my great good fortunes—and inspirations—in life. And again, without saddling them with responsibility for its shortcomings, they have contributed importantly to *Churn*'s development.

And my good fortune does not end there. I, and the thinking in *Churn*, have benefited mightily from many, many years of breakfast and dinner table conversations and a shared moral and intellectual vision with my late wife, Dorothy Steele, and from abiding friendships, such as those with Robert Radford and Duayne Fulton, who have, for many years, helped me think about and understand the issues taken up in this book. And without the loving support of my current partner, Alina Matsa, in whose house much of this book was written, *Churn* would have come to pass much more slowly, if at all. They have my immense gratitude.

Drawing closer to the writing and production of *Churn*, I've had equally good fortune in the editorial support I've gotten from W. W. Norton, especially from my friend and editor Robert Weil, whose advice, patience, encouragement, and just plain brilliance have helped immeasurably. His and Roby Harrington's yearslong encouragement has a lot to do with this book's eventually getting done. (Roby, a retired Norton editor, brought my earlier book, *Whistling Vivaldi*, through the publishing process.) Bob is a genius at what he does, and it has been a

ACKNOWLEDGMENTS

great pleasure and honor to work with him on every aspect of this project. As it has also been to work with Janet Byrne, who Bob was able to entice into being its copyeditor. She, too, is a master at what she does. I want to also thank Justin Cahill from Norton's textbook division for his invaluable comments on an earlier draft and Luke Swann for his careful management of the production process. And finally, I cannot imagine being better supported than I have been by Tina Bennett, my longtime agent. She is a brilliant manager of the connection between business particulars and the intellectual vision of a project. She knows so well how to keep the former true to the latter.

To the extent that this book fulfills that vision, it is in large part due to this thoughtful community of support that I have, for so long, had the good fortune to be part of.

REFERENCES

PROLOGUE

Markus, H. R., C. M. Steele, and D. M. Steele. "Colorblindness as a Barrier to Inclusion: Assimilation and Nonimmigrant Minorities." *Daedalus* 129 (2000), 233–59.

INTRODUCTION

Boyce, J. M., D. Pittet, and the Healthcare Infection Control Practices Advisory Committee. "Guideline for Hand Hygiene in Health-Care Settings: Recommendations of the Healthcare Infection Control Practices Advisory Committee and the HICPAC/SHEA/APIC/IDSA Hand Hygiene Task Force." *Morbidity and Mortality Weekly Report* 51 (2002), 1–44.

Frankenberg, E., J. Ee, J. B. Ayscue, and G. Orfield. "Harming Our Common Future: America's Segregated Schools 65 Years After *Brown*." UCLA Civil Rights Project. May 10, 2019.

CHAPTER 1: WHAT IS CHURN?

Faulkner, W. *Requiem for a Nun*. Random House, 1951.

Ishiguro, K. *My Twentieth Century Evening and Other Small Breakthroughs: The Nobel Lecture*. Knopf, 2017.

Reddit (2019). "I fear of being called racist, does that make me a racist." https://www.reddit.com/r/socialjustice101/comments/c50ndz/i_fear_of_being_called_racist_does_that_make_me_a.

Richeson, J. A., and J. N. Shelton. "When Prejudice Does Not Pay: Effects of Interracial Contact on Executive Functioning." *Psychological Science* 14 (2003), 287–90.

Richeson, J. A., and J. N. Shelton. "Negotiating Interracial Interactions: Costs, Consequences, and Possibilities." *Current Directions in Psychological Science* 16 (2007), 313–20.

Schmader, T., M. Johns, and C. Forbes. "An Integrated Process Model of Stereotype Threat Effects on Performance." *Psychological Review* 115 (2008), 336–56.

Steele, C. M., and J. Aronson. "Stereotype Threat and the Intellectual Test Performance of African Americans." *Journal of Personality and Social Psychology* 69 (1995), 797–811.

REFERENCES

Stop AAPI Hate. "The State of Anti-AA/PI Hate in 2023: From Pain to Power—Asian American and Pacific Islander Activation in the Face of Hate. Inaugural National Survey and Reporting Center Findings." September 2024.

Stroop, J. R. "Studies of Interference in Serial Verbal Reactions." *Journal of Experimental Psychology* 18 (1935), 643–62.

Valerio, Mirna, quotes from *Rich Roll* (podcast), episode 536, August 3, 2020.

CHAPTER 2: WHERE DOES CHURN COME FROM?
Alexander, E. *The Trayvon Generation*. Grand Central Publishing, 2022.

Tajfel, H. "Experiments in Intergroup Discrimination." *Scientific American* 223 (1970), 96–103.

Tajfel, H., M. Billig, R. P. Bundy, and C. Flament. "Social Categorization and Intergroup Behaviour." *European Journal of Social Psychology* 1 (1971), 149–78.

Wilkerson, I. *Caste: The Origins of Our Discontents*. Random House, 2020.

CHAPTER 3: CHURN HAS AN ANTIDOTE
Hetey, R. C., M. G. Hamedani, H. R. Markus, and J. L. Eberhardt. "'When the Cruiser Lights Come On': Using the Science of Bias and Culture to Combat Racial Disparities in Policing." *Daedalus* 153 (2024), 123–50.

Samuels, R., and T. Olorunnipa. *His Name Is George Floyd: One Man's Life and the Struggle for Racial Justice*. Viking, 2022.

Schul, Y., R. Mayo, and E. Burnstein. "Encoding Under Trust and Distrust: The Spontaneous Activation of Incongruent Cognitions." *Journal of Personality and Social Psychology* 86 (2004), 668–79.

CHAPTER 4: BEING WISE, NOT COLOR-BLIND
Borman, G. D., J. Grigg, and P. Hanselman. "An Effort to Close Achievement Gaps at Scale Through Self-Affirmation." *Educational Evaluation and Policy Analysis* 38 (2016), 21–42.

Borman, G. D., J. Grigg, C. S. Rozek, P. Hanselman, and N. A. Dewey. "Self-Affirmation Effects Are Produced by School Context, Student Engagement with the Intervention, and Time: Lessons from a District-Wide Implementation." *Psychological Science* 29 (2018), 1773–84.

Borman, G. D., Y. Choi, and G. J. Hall. "The Impacts of a Brief Middle-School Self-Affirmation Intervention Help Propel African American and Latino Students Through High School." *Journal of Educational Psychology* 113 (2021), 605–20.

Cohen, G. L., J. Garcia, N. Apfel, and A. Master. "Reducing the Racial Achievement Gap: A Social-Psychological Intervention." *Science* 313 (2006), 1307–10.

REFERENCES

Cohen, G. L., C. M. Steele, and L. D. Ross. "The Mentor's Dilemma: Providing Critical Feedback Across the Racial Divide." *Personality and Social Psychology Bulletin* 25 (1999), 1302–18.

Crocker, J., and B. Major. "Social Stigma and Self-Esteem: The Self-Protective Properties of Stigma." *Psychological Review* 96 (1989), 608–30.

Dweck, C. S. *Mindset—Updated Edition: Changing the Way You Think to Fulfil Your Potential.* Ballantine Books, 2017.

Goffman, E. *Stigma: Notes on the Management of Spoiled Identity.* Penguin Books, 1963.

Heckman, D. "Still Miles Ahead." *Los Angeles Times*, September 1, 1996.

Lepper, M. R., M. Woolverton, D. L. Mumme, and J.-L. Gurtner. "Motivational Techniques of Expert Human Tutors: Lessons for the Design of Computer-Based Tutors." In S. P. Lajoie and S. J. Derry, eds., *Computers as Cognitive Tools.* Routledge, 1993.

Sherman, D. K., et al. "Deflecting the Trajectory and Changing the Narrative: How Self-Affirmation Affects Academic Performance and Motivation under Identity Threat." *Journal of Personality and Social Psychology* 104 (2013), 591.

CHAPTER 5: TRUST IN THE FACE OF POWER

Chenoweth, E., and M. J. Stephan. *Why Civil Resistance Works: The Strategic Logic of Nonviolent Conflict.* Columbia University Press, 2011.

Coates, T. "My President Was Black." *The Atlantic*, January/February 2017.

Ditlmann, R. K., V. Purdie-Vaughns, J. F. Dovidio, and M. J. Naft. "The Implicit Power Motive in Intergroup Dialogues About the History of Slavery." *Journal of Personality and Social Psychology* 112 (2017), 116–35.

Klein, C. "How Selma's 'Bloody Sunday' Became a Turning Point in the Civil Rights Movement." History.com, March 6, 2015.

Mooijman, M. "Power Dynamics and the Reciprocation of Trust and Distrust." *Journal of Personality and Social Psychology* 125 (2023), 779–802.

Nicholasen, M. "Q&A with Erica Chenoweth." *The Harvard Gazette*, February 4, 2019.

CHAPTER 6: MAKING SCHOOL AND WORK SETTINGS WISE

Alexander, E. *The Trayvon Generation.* Grand Central Publishing, 2022.

Cheryan, S., V. C. Plaut, P. G. Davies, and C. M. Steele. "Ambient Belonging: How Stereotypical Cues Impact Gender Participation in Computer Science." *Journal of Personality and Social Psychology* 97 (2009), 1045–60.

Marsh, C. *The Beloved Community: How Faith Shapes Social Justice, from the Civil Rights Movement to Today.* Basic Books, 2005.

REFERENCES

Murphy, M. C. *Cultures of Growth*. Simon & Schuster, 2024.

Murphy, M. C., C. M. Steele, and J. J. Gross. "Signaling Threat: How Situational Cues Affect Women in Math, Science, and Engineering Settings." *Psychological Science* 18 (2007), 879–85.

Notes from personal communication (2022) with Kelly Madrone on her interview with Jayshree Seth of 3M.

Purdie-Vaughns, V., C. M. Steele, P. G. Davies, R. Ditlmann, and J. R. Crosby. "Social Identity Contingencies: How Diversity Cues Signal Threat or Safety for African Americans in Mainstream Institutions." *Journal of Personality and Social Psychology* 94 (2008), 615–30.

Stephens, N. M., S. A. Fryberg, H. R. Markus, C. S. Johnson, and R. Covarrubias. "Unseen Disadvantage: How American Universities' Focus on Independence Undermines the Academic Performance of First-Generation College Students." *Journal of Personality and Social Psychology* 102 (2012), 1178–97.

CHAPTER 7: MAKING INSTITUTIONS WISE

Fisher, A. J., et al. "Structure and Belonging: Pathways to Success for Underrepresented Minority and Women PhD Students in STEM Fields." *PloS ONE* 14 (2019), e0209279.

Glass, D. C., and J. E. Singer. *Urban Stress: Experiments on Noise and Social Stressors*. Academic Press, 1972.

Gumbel, A. *Won't Lose This Dream: How an Upstart Urban University Rewrote the Rules of a Broken System*. The New Press, 2020.

Mendoza-Denton, R., et al. "Differences in STEM Doctoral Publication by Ethnicity, Gender and Academic Field at a Larger Public Research University." *PloS ONE* 12 (2017), e0174296.

CHAPTER 8: MAKING GUIDING PARADIGMS WISE

Bowles, S., and H. Gintis. *Schooling in Capitalist America: Educational Reform and the Contradictions of Economic Life*. Basic Books, 1976.

Cohen, G. L., J. Garcia, N. Apfel, and A. Master. "Reducing the Racial Achievement Gap: A Social-Psychological Intervention." *Science* 313 (2006), 1307–10.

Cohen, G. L., J. Garcia, V. Purdie-Vaughns, N. Apfel, and P. Brzustoski. "Recursive Processes in Self-Affirmation: Intervening to Close the Minority Achievement Gap." *Science* 324 (2009), 400–3.

Dewey, J. *Democracy and Education: An Introduction to the Philosophy of Education*. Macmillan, 1916.

Doan, S., E. D. Steiner, A. Woo, and R. Pandey. *State of the American Teacher Survey: 2024 Technical Documentation and Survey Results* (RR-A1108-11). RAND Corporation, 2024.

REFERENCES

Durlak, J. A., R. P. Weissberg, A. B. Dymnicki, R. D. Taylor, and K. B. Schellinger. "The Impact of Enhancing Students' Social and Emotional Learning: A Meta-Analysis of School-Based Universal Interventions." *Child Development* 82 (2011), 405–32.

Every Student Succeeds Act, Public Law No. 114-95, enacted December 10, 2015.

Heckman, J., R. Pinto, and P. Savelyev. "Understanding the Mechanisms Through Which an Influential Early Childhood Program Boosted Adult Outcomes." *American Economic Review* 103 (2013), 2052–86.

Jackson, C. K. "What Do Test Scores Miss? The Importance of Teacher Effects on Non-Test-Score Outcomes." NBER Working Paper No. 22226. National Bureau of Economic Research, 2016.

Kahn, J. "Can Emotional Intelligence Be Taught?" *New York Times Magazine*, September 15, 2013.

Kidd, C., H. Palmeri, and R. N. Aslin. "Rational Snacking: Young Children's Decision-Making on the Marshmallow Task Is Moderated by Beliefs About Environmental Reliability." *Cognition* 126 (2013), 109–14.

Kirp, D. L. *Improbable Scholars: The Rebirth of a Great American School System and a Strategy for America's Schools.* Oxford University Press, 2013.

Kuhn, T. S. *The Structure of Scientific Revolutions*, 1st ed. University of Chicago Press, 1962.

Mischel, W., and E. B. Ebbesen. "Attention in Delay of Gratification." *Journal of Personality and Social Psychology* 16 (1970), 329–37.

Nelson, C. A., III, and M. A. Sheridan. "Lessons from Neuroscience Research for Understanding Causal Links Between Family and Neighborhood Characteristics and Educational Outcomes." In G. J. Duncan and R. J. Murnane, eds., *Whither Opportunity? Rising Inequality, Schools, and Children's Life Chances.* Russell Sage Foundation, 2011.

OECD. PISA (Programme for International Student Assessment) 2012 Results, Volume II: *Excellence Through Equity: Giving Every Student the Chance to Succeed.* OECD Publishing, Paris, 2013.

OECD. PISA 2022 Results, Volume I: *The State of Learning and Equity in Education.* OECD Publishing, Paris, 2023.

Okonofua, J. A., D. Paunesku, and G. M. Walton. "Brief Intervention to Encourage Empathic Discipline Cuts Suspension Rates in Half Among Adolescents." *Proceedings of the National Academy of Sciences* 113 (2016), 5221–26.

Pianta, R. C., J. Belsky, R. Houts, and F. Morrison. "Opportunities to Learn in America's Elementary Classrooms." *Science* 315 (2007), 1795–96.

Southern Education Foundation. "A New Majority: Low Income Students Now a Majority in the Nation's Public Schools." Research Bulletin, 2015.

REFERENCES

Walton, G. M., and G. L. Cohen. "A Brief SocialBelonging Intervention Improves Academic and Health Outcomes of Minority Students." *Science* 331 (2011), 1447–51.

CHAPTER 9: GOING FORWARD

Allport, G. W. *The Nature of Prejudice*. 25th Anniversary Edition. Basic Books, 1979.

Aronson, J., C. B. Fried, and C. Good. "Reducing the Effects of Stereotype Threat on African American College Students by Shaping Theories of Intelligence." *Journal of Experimental Social Psychology* 38 (2002), 113–25.

Dweck, C. S. *Mindset—Updated Edition: Changing the Way You Think to Fulfil Your Potential*. Ballantine Books, 2017.

Gumbel, A. *Won't Lose This Dream: How an Upstart Urban University Rewrote the Rules of a Broken System*. The New Press, 2020.

Marsh, C. *The Beloved Community: How Faith Shapes Social Justice, from the Civil Rights Movement to Today*. Basic Books, 2005.

Moses, R. P., and C. E. Cobb Jr. *Radical Equations: Math Literacy and Civil Rights*. Beacon Press, 2001.

Murphy, M. C. *Cultures of Growth*. Simon & Schuster, 2024.

Notes from personal communication (2022) with Kelly Madrone on her interview with Greyston Bakery.

Ross, L. "The Intuitive Psychologist and His Shortcomings: Distortions in the Attribution Process." In L. Berkowitz, ed., *Advances in Experimental Social Psychology*, Volume 10, 173–220. Academic Press, 1977.

Skoog-Hoffman, A., et al. "Social and Emotional Learning in US Schools." RAND Corporation, 2024.

Stephens, N. M., S. A. Fryberg, H. R. Markus, C. S. Johnson, and R Covarrubias. "Unseen Disadvantage: How American Universities' Focus on Independence Undermines the Academic Performance of First-Generation College Students." *Journal of Personality and Social Psychology* 102 (2012), 1178–97.

Walton, G. M. *Ordinary Magic: The Science of How We Can Achieve Big Change with Small Acts*. Harmony, 2025.

Yeager, D. S., and C. S. Dweck. "What Can Be Learned from Growth Mindset Controversies?" *American Psychologist* 75 (2020), 1269–84.

CODA: AND EVERYONE CAN DO IT

Lerner, M. J., and C. H. Simmons. "Observer's Reaction to the 'Innocent Victim': Compassion or Rejection?" *Journal of Personality and Social Psychology* 4 (1966), 203–10.

INDEX

Note: Footnotes are indicated by *n* after the page number.

actor's perspective, 156–59
affirmative action, 3–4, 38, 50
African Americans
   in Cohen feedback study, 64–66, 73, 76–77, 146
   Georgia State University and, 111, 117, 118, 120
   lack of trust in diverse settings, 75–76
   in parent-teacher conferences (*see* parent-teacher conferences)
   power relations and trust, 76–77, 82–84
   self-affirming exercise and, 67–70, 145, 146
   stereotype threat in test taking, 15–17, 19
   See also specific topics and individuals
Alexander, Elizabeth, 37, 92
Allport, Gordon, 155, 173
ambiguity
   attributional ambiguity, 66
   of coping in important settings, 106, 108–11
   of feedback, 66, 77
   red buttons for reducing, 108, 110–11, 125, 128
   reduction at Berkeley Chemistry, 122–24, 125–26, 128
   reduction at Georgia State University (GSU), 117, 120, 128
"America's expansion of opportunity project," 2–3
Apfel, Nancy, 67, 145
Arendt, Hannah, 29
Aronson, Joshua, 15–16, 146, 150
Asian grandmother's fear of being pushed to the ground, 24, 37
Aslin, Richard, 141
Aydlett, Billy, 144

balanced and unbalanced video experiment, 90–92
banality of evil, 29
Becker, Mark, 114
behavior as driver of attitudes, 52
"beloved community" concept, 102–3, 154–55
Berkeley Chemistry
   ambiguity reduction, 122–24, 125–26, 128
   approach to inclusion, 127–29, 130, 167
   churn-reducing structures and supports, 125–26, 130, 166, 167, 169
   clear expectations in graduate program, 122–23, 124

INDEX

Berkeley Chemistry (*continued*)
  incrementalism and, 175
  orientation program for new students, 122, 130, 169
  underrepresented minorities, publication by, 124–25, 126
  wise strategy to develop academic talent, 128–29
bias
  associations between identities and tendencies, 44–45
  corrosive to diversity, 43–44
  intergroup contact effect on, 12
  mitigation of, 45n
  in schools, 149–50
  unconscious biases, 5, 44, 45n
  See also prejudice
Borman, Geoffrey, 69
Bowles, Samuel, 149
Bronx Tale, A (movie), 39–41, 44
Brown v. Board of Education, 3, 4, 33, 50
Bryant, Carolyn, 27

Calhoun-Brown, Allison, 114
Calogero (movie character), 39–41, 48, 49
Caste (Wilkerson), 31–33, 34, 35, 56, 57, 59, 72
character traits as predictors of life outcomes, 136, 141, 142–43
Chauvin, Derek, 45
Chenoweth, Erica, 87–88
Cheryan, Sapna, 93, 94
childhood poverty
  challenge of inclusion in schools, 134
  decreasing churn of low-income students, 138
  deprivation and low social status, 133–34, 137–38
  effects on brain and nervous system development, 140
  and Kaylie, 132–33
  poverty-driven impediments to school success, 139–43, 148–49
  and social-psychological aspects of schooling, 143, 144–45
  statistics, 134, 149
  and stereotype threat in schools, 140, 145
  test score gaps between rich and poor students, 135–36
  and Tyler, 132–34, 137–38, 140–41, 142–43, 145, 147–48
churn, generally
  caused by stereotype threat, 9, 10, 66–67
  culture mismatch and, 95–97
  defined, 9, 10
  interference with performance, 15–19, 20, 22–23
  in parent-teacher conferences, 7, 35–36, 176
  prejudice reduced by reducing churn, 52, 174
  and threat of isms, 173–74
  See also stereotype threat
Civil Rights Acts of 1964 and 1965, 3, 33, 38, 50
civil rights movement
  "beloved community" concept, 102–3, 154–55
  and *Brown v. Board of Education*, 3, 4, 33, 50
  concern of retaliatory violence in 1950s and 1960s, 102
  Freedom Rides, 102
  legislation passed, 3, 33, 38, 50, 86–87, 160
  national commitment to integration, 26, 33–34, 37–38
  Selma, Alabama, protest march, 84–86, 88
  trust and trust-building, 84, 86–87

INDEX

violent *vs.* nonviolent campaigns, 87–88, 102
voter registration drives, 102, 160
wiseness, 87
Clark, Douglas, 123
Classroom Assessment Scoring System (CLASS), 148
Cloud, John, 85
clutter, effects on men and women, 93–94
Coates, Ta-Nehisi, 71, 75, 81–82
cognitive-accountability paradigm, 134–37, 138–39, 141, 143, 147, 149, 151–52
Cohen, Geoffrey, 64–66, 67–69, 73, 76–77, 145, 146
Cohn-Vargas, Becki, 146
College of Chemistry, University of California at Berkeley. *See* Berkeley Chemistry
colleges and universities
 achievement gap of middle-and working-class students, 95–96
 ambiguity and lack of program structure, 121
 culture mismatch and churn, 95–97
 graduate program at Ohio State, 89–90
 painting of Elihu Yale, 92
 reducing identity threat for students, 146–47
 remediate-to-assimilate approaches, 127–28
 underrepresented minorities in STEM fields, publication by, 124–25, 126–27
 welcome letters and college culture, 96–97, 98, 164–65, 170
 See also Berkeley Chemistry; Georgia State University; institutions; school and work settings; schools
color-blindness
 being "cool" compared to, 55–56

good intentions and, 56–57
identity overlooked, 56, 73
limitations of this approach, 44, 48, 58, 73
as standard of fairness, 44
as strategy for identity-integrated society, 44
Complete College America, 112
Covarrubias, Rebecca, 95
COVID-19 pandemic, 37
Crocker, Jennifer, 66
cues audit to identify and address identity threat, 99–101, 163

Davies, Paul, 93
Davis, Miles, 54–56, 57, 176
deescalating scripts for police to use, 45n
DEI (diversity, equity, and inclusion), 4, 38
Dewey, John, 149
Ditlmann, Ruth, 82
diversity
 bias as corrosive to, 43–44
 and culture and structure in STEM PhD programs, 126–27
 defined, 34
 national commitment to, 37–38
 racialization by, 36
 and stress, 11–12
 and threat of race-based violence, 37
 through law and regulations, 50
"door" test in *A Bronx Tale*, 40–41, 43, 48, 49
dot-estimation experiment, 29–30, 63, 160, 173, 175
Dovidio, John, 82, 173
Du Bois, W. E. B., 155
Dweck, Carol, 61, 146

Eberhardt, Jennifer, 45n, 173
essay feedback experiment, 64–66, 73, 76–77

INDEX

Evans, Gil, 54–56, 57, 176
Every Student Succeeds Act (ESSA), 135, 151
expert tutors, 60–63, 150

Fair Housing Act of 1968, 33
Faulkner, William, 18
Fisher, Aaron, 126, 127
Floyd, George, 28, 45–48, 49, 151
Floyd, Missy, 46
forgetting and churn, 10
forgetting-*versus*-remembering tension, 10, 14, 72, 74–75
Freedom Rides, 102
Freud, Sigmund, 155
Fryberg, Stephanie, 95

Gandhi, 84
Garcia, Julio, 67, 145
Georgia State University (GSU)
  about, 111–12, 156
  ambiguity reduction, 117, 120, 128
  approach to inclusion, 127–29, 130, 167
  approach to student success, 112–14, 119
  churn-reducing structures and supports, 130, 162–63, 166, 167, 169
  data and data analytics used for change, 114–15, 117–18, 119–20, 175
  dropout problem, 113, 127–29, 161–62, 163
  graduation rates, 112, 117–18, 161–62
  HOPE scholarships for low-income students, 157–58, 159, 170
  incrementalism, 170, 175
  Keep HOPE Alive (KHA), 157–58
  normalization of identity differences, 118, 162
  orientation program for new students, 115–16, 130
  Pell Grants, 116, 120
  Scholarship Resource Center, 115
  Strategic Plan, 113–14
  Student Advisement Center (SAC), 116–17
  student participation in STEM courses, 118–19
  wise strategy to develop academic talent, 113, 128–29
  See also Renick, Timothy
Gintis, Herbert, 149
Glass, David, 108, 110
Goffman, Erving, 55, 57, 60, 62, 64
Graduate Record Examinations (GRE), 16–17, 18–19
Greyston Bakery, in Yonkers, New York, 165–66
Gross, James, 90–91
GSU. *See* Georgia State University
Gumbel, Andrew, 113, 115, 157

hands, color of author's, 89–90, 92, 99
handwashing by hospital staff, 1, 2
hate crimes, 24
Heckman, James, 136
Hiram College, 106–8, 110, 121
historically Black colleges and universities (HBCUs), 19, 120
Holloman, Darryl, 115
HOPE Scholarship program for low-income students, 157–58, 159, 170
hospital-acquired infections, 1, 2
hostile work environment, 90

identification paradigm, 147, 152
identities
  overlooked by color-blindness, 56
  stratification in social order, 32–33

INDEX

and threat of isms, 173–74
threat of negative stereotypes about,
  6–7
in Wilkerson's *Caste* play, 31–33, 34,
  35, 56, 57, 59, 72
identity-blindness, 5, 44–45, 47–48,
  98–99, 143
See also color-blindness
identity contingencies, 45–48
identity threat
  Asian grandmother's fear of being
    pushed to the ground, 24, 37
  churn caused by, 9, 15–16
  at college, 109
  cues audit to identify and address,
    99–101, 163
  defined, 9
  diversity and, 15–16, 36
  interpersonal judgments compared to,
    24, 25
  life-shaping effects of, 24–25
  paradigms and, 131–32
  reducing, for college students, 146–47,
    163
  self-affirmation and, 68–70, 145, 146
  triggered by settings, 93
Immigration and Nationality Act of
  1965, 33
Improbable Scholars (Kirp), 150
inclusion
  Berkeley Chemistry approach, 127–29,
    130, 167
  childhood poverty as challenge, 134
  DEI (diversity, equity, and inclusion),
    4, 38
  Georgia State University approach,
    127–29, 130, 167
  tug-of-war between inclusion and
    resistance, 3–5, 38
  units of society as agents of, 127–28
  wise model of, 128–29

institutions
  ambiguity of coping in, 106, 108–11
  data and data analytics value in
    change, 114–15, 117–18, 119–20
  developmental approach to inclusion,
    129–30
  prejudice and, 52–53
  units of society as agents of inclusion,
    127–28
  See also Berkeley Chemistry; Georgia
    State University
Ishiguro, Kazuo, 9–10

Jackson, Kirabo, 136
Jensen, Arthur, 89
Jim Crow segregation, 3, 85, 87
Johnson, Camille, 95
Judgment at Nuremberg (movie), 86
just world, belief in, 171–72

Kahn, Jennifer, 144
Kaylie, 132–33
Keep HOPE Alive (KHA), 157–58
Kidd, Celeste, 141
King, Martin Luther Jr., 84, 102, 154
Kirp, David, 150
Klein, Christopher, 84
Kuhn, Thomas, 135

Ladson Billings, Gloria, 146
Lepper, Mark, 62–63
Lerner, Melvin, 171, 172
Lewis, John, 84, 85, 154
long-distance hikers, 14, 20, 24
low-income students. *See* childhood
  poverty

Major, Brenda, 66
Markus, Hazel Rose, 95
Marsh, Charles, 102
marshmallow experiments, 141–42

INDEX

mass change campaigns, violent *vs.*
nonviolent, 87–88
Master, Allison, 67, 145
Mendoza-Denton, Rodolfo, 124
Mischel, Walter, 141
Mooijman, Marlon, 78–81
"More Teaching Less Testing" bill, 151
Moses, Robert, 160–61, 162, 176
Mullainathan, Sendhil, 140
Murphy, Mary, 90–92, 97–98, 99, 103, 146, 163
musicians auditioned from behind a screen, 5, 45n, 174

Naft, Michael, 82
Neal, Pat, 106–9, 110–11, 116, 128, 158
Nelson, Charles, 140
No Child Left Behind (NCLB), 135
non-cognitive traits as predictors of success, 136, 141, 142–43
nonviolent *vs.* violent mass change campaigns, 87–88
Nuremberg trials, 28

Obama, Barack, 71, 75, 81–82, 83, 84
observer's perspective, 155–56, 157, 161
Okonofua, Jason, 146, 152
Open Hiring model, 165–66
Organization for Economic Cooperation and Development (OECD), 134, 135
over-dot-estimators, 29–30, 31, 32, 63

Palmeri, Holly, 141
paradigms
    in ancient astronomy, 131
    cognitive-accountability paradigm, 134–37, 138–39, 141, 143, 147, 149, 151–52
    defined, 131
    identification paradigm, 147, 152
    and identity threat, 131–32

parent-teacher conferences
    churn in, 7, 35–36, 176
    mistrust and trust in diverse setting, 34, 75
    overview, xi–xiii
    prejudice and, 35–36, 43–44, 52
    stereotype threat, 6, 18, 35–36, 58–59
    trust building, 176
    wiseness in, 58–59
Paunesku, David, 152
Perry Preschool Project in Ypsilanti, Michigan, 136
Pianta, Robert, 148–49
PISA (Programme for International Student Assessment), 135, 149
Plaut, Victoria, 93
Poor Kids (TV documentary), 132–34
poverty in childhood. *See* childhood poverty
prejudice
    author's introduction to the word, 27–28
    difficulty of changing, 51
    dividing people into groups, 30–31, 174
    educational interventions to reduce, 174
    from escalation of ordinary human tendencies, 29
    explanatory narratives, 30–31
    and institutions, 52–53
    musicians auditioned from behind a screen, 5, 45n, 174
    and parent-teacher conferences, 35–36, 43–44, 52
    reduced by reducing churn, 52, 174
    unconscious biases, effect on behavior, 5
    See also bias
procedural justice, 125–26
Purdie Greenaway, Valerie, 67, 67n, 82, 146
Purdie-Vaughns, Valerie, 67n
    See also Purdie Greenaway, Valerie

INDEX

red buttons for ambiguity reduction, 108, 110–11, 125, 128
Reddit post by young white man, 13–14, 15, 18
remembering
   caused by stereotypes, 24
   churn from, 10
   and color of hands, 89–90, 92, 99
   remembering-*versus*-forgetting tension, 10, 14, 72, 74–75
Renick, Timothy
   approach to student success at GSU, 112–14, 116, 119, 157–58, 162–63
   data used for institutional change, 114–15, 118–19
   education and early career, 112, 156
   and HOPE scholarships for low-income students, 157–58, 159, 170
   Keep HOPE Alive (KHA), 157–58
   seeing as a strategy, 160, 162, 163
   on student participation in STEM courses, 118–19
   wiseness, 176
Reynolds, Frank, 86
Richeson, Jennifer, 11–12
Richeson-Shelton experiments, 11–12, 13
Rock, Chris, 48
Ross, Lee, 64
Royce, Josiah, 102

Scarcity (Mullainathan and Shafir), 140
Schmader, Toni, 21
school and work settings
   graduate program at Ohio State, 89–90
   hostile work environment, 90
   and painting of Elihu Yale, 92
   stereotypes about African Americans' intellectual abilities, 89–90
   3M, culture of innovation, 97–98, 99, 101
   See also colleges and universities; institutions; settings of society
Schooling in Capitalist America (Bowles and Gintis), 149
schools
   basic skills curricula, 137, 138, 139, 143, 148–49
   Brown v. Board of Education and, 3, 4, 33, 50
   cognitive-accountability paradigm in, 134–37, 138–39, 141, 143, 147, 151
   cognitive remediations, 143, 149–50
   decreasing churn of low-income students, 138
   and empathic mindset of teachers, 152–53
   importance of trust in, 134, 137–38, 141–42, 147, 150, 152
   low-income students and stereotype threat, 140, 145
   non-cognitive traits as predictors of success, 136, 141, 142–43
   poverty-driven impediments to school success, 139–43, 148–49
   school reform, principles of, 150–51
   segregation today, 4, 33, 49
   social-emotional learning (SEL) practices, 144–45, 148
   social-psychological aspects of schooling, 143, 144–45, 147, 163
   stereotype threat and Black students, 16–18, 21
   See also colleges and universities; parent-teacher conferences
Schul, Yaacov, 41–42
seeing, welcoming, and supporting
   for maintaining a sense of justice in the world, 172
   in parent-teacher conference, 176–78
   seeing as a trust-building strategy, 160–63, 169, 170, 172, 174–75, 176

INDEX

seeing, welcoming, and supporting (*continued*)
   supporting as a trust-building strategy, 162, 166–69, 170, 172, 174–75, 176, 178
   welcoming as a trust-building strategy, 164–66, 169–70, 172, 174–75, 176, 177–78, 179
self-affirmation, 68–70, 145, 146
self-affirming exercise, 67–70, 145, 146
Selma, Alabama, protest march, 84–86, 88
Seth, Jayshree, 98
settings of society
   agency of, 92–93
   building trust in diverse settings, 131, 146, 164
   churn increased by, 7, 93–94
   cues audit, 99–101, 163
   evaluating features of, 99–101, 103–4
   lack of trust in diverse settings, 34, 75, 114, 126
   mobilizing for integration, 50–51
   social tension in diverse settings, 35
   stereotype threat in diverse settings, 6–7, 21, 34–36, 57–58
   See also school and work settings
Shafir, Eldar, 140
Shelton, Nicole, 11–12
Sheridan, Margaret, 140
Sherman, David, 146
Simmons, Carolyn, 171, 172
Singer, Jerome, 108, 110
SNCC (Student Nonviolent Coordinating Committee), 85, 102, 160
social-emotional learning (SEL) practices, 144–45, 148
social-psychological aspects of schooling, 143, 144–45, 147, 163
social tension in diverse settings, 35

spoiled identity, 55, 62
Steele, Claude M.
   family background, 2–3
   in graduate program at Ohio State, 89–90
   high school and Hiram College, 105–8, 110, 121
   introduction to the word "prejudice," 27–28
Steele, Dorothy, 146
Stephan, Maria, 87–88
Stephens, Nicole, 95, 99, 164–65
stereotypes
   about African Americans' intellectual abilities, 89–90
   actor's perspective, 156–59
   attached to roles in parent-teacher conferences, xi, xii
   from explanatory narratives, 30–31
   known by anyone, 23–24
   observer's perspective, 155–56, 157, 161
   wiseness in spite of, 58–59
stereotype threat
   actor's perspective, 156–59
   and Black students, 16–18, 21
   churn caused by, 9, 10, 66–67
   defined, 10
   in diverse settings, 6–7, 21, 34–36, 57–58
   interference with performance, 15–19, 20, 22–23
   and intergroup empathy, 25–26
   interpersonal judgments compared to, 23–24, 25
   as motivation to improve performance, 22
   observer's perspective, 155–56
   in parent-teacher conferences, 6, 18, 35–36, 58–59
   as a predicament, 18–19, 22–23, 26

INDEX

research on effects of, 20–21
threat of being seen as racist, 13–14
Stigma (Goffman), 55
stigma and stigmatization, 55–56, 57, 128, 162, 167
Stone Mountain in Georgia, 92–93
strategy *vs.* tactics, 169–70
stress
   of churn, 9, 12
   college stress, 146, 157
   diversity and, 11–12
   effect of poverty, 139
   of living in a city, 108–9
   Stroop test and, 11–12
Stroop, John Ridley, 11
Stroop test, 11–12
Structure of Scientific Revolutions, The (Kuhn), 135
Student Nonviolent Coordinating Committee (SNCC), 85, 102, 160
Students for Fair Admissions v. President and Fellows of Harvard College, 4, 50
supporting
   guidelines for, 167–69
   as a trust-building strategy, 162, 166–69, 170, 172, 174–75, 176, 178

tactics *vs.* strategy, 169–70
Tajfel dot-estimation experiment, 29–30, 63, 160, 173, 175
Tajfel, Henri, 29–30
tension between different identities, as focus of book, 1–2
Testing Reduction Act (North Carolina), 151
test-related anxieties among white students, 17n
tests in cognitive-accountability paradigm, 134–37, 151
threat of negative stereotypes. *See* stereotype threat

3M, culture of innovation, 97–98, 99, 101
Till, Emmett, 27–28
Trayvon Generation, The (Alexander), 37, 92
trust and trust-building
   and ability to delay gratification, 141–42
   accepting dominant meanings in a situation, 41–42
   advantage of focusing on, 51–52
   as antidote to churn, 40–41, 178
   building trust in diverse settings, 131, 146, 164
   civil rights movement, 84, 86–87
   data and data analytics in large organizations, 114–15
   "door" test in *A Bronx Tale*, 40–41, 43, 48, 49
   and focus of *Churn*, 2, 155, 174
   game of trust, 78–80
   identity-based disadvantages and, 49–50
   incrementalism and, 170, 175
   leadership by the more empowered, 76–77, 176
   from the less powerful in diverse setting, 74–76
   mistrust in diverse setting, 34, 75, 114, 126
   Obama and, 71, 75, 81, 82, 83, 84
   and personal connection, 161, 176–77
   perspective-taking and, 155–60
   power relations and trust, 76–77, 79–81, 82–84
   in schools, importance of, 134, 137–38, 141–42, 147, 150, 152
   seeing as a trust-building strategy, 160–63, 169, 170, 172, 174–75, 176
   signals that evoke trust, 43, 49, 138
   as strategy for identity-integrated society, 49–50
   supporting as a trust-building strategy, 162, 166–69, 170, 172, 174–75, 176, 178

INDEX

trust and trust-building (*continued*)
  welcoming as a trust-building strategy, 164–66, 169–70, 172, 174–75, 176, 177–78, 179
  who should be responsible for, 72
  wise feedback and, 73, 76–77, 114
  wiseness and, 58–60, 64, 71, 75–77
tug-of-war between inclusion and resistance, 3–5, 38
tutors wisely overlooking reputation, 60–63, 150
Tyler, 132–34, 137–38, 140–41, 142–43, 145, 147–48

UC Berkeley College of Chemistry. *See* Berkeley Chemistry
ultrarunners and long-distance hikers, 14, 19
unconscious biases, 5, 44, 45*n*
under-dot-estimators, 29–30, 31, 32, 63
Union City, New Jersey, schools, 152
units of society as agents of inclusion, 127–28
University Innovation Alliance, 119

Valerio, Mirna "the Mirnavator," 14–15, 18, 19–20, 21–22, 23–24, 25, 106
violent *vs.* nonviolent mass change campaigns, 87–88, 102
Voting Rights Act of 1965, 33, 86–87, 160

Walton, Gregory, 146, 152
welcome letters and college culture, 96–97, 98, 164–65, 170
welcoming as a trust-building strategy, 164–66, 169–70, 172, 174–75, 176, 177–78, 179
Whistling Vivaldi (Steele), 6
Wilkerson, Isabel, 31

Wilkerson's *Caste* play, 31–33, 34, 35, 56, 57, 59, 72
Williams, Hosea, 85
Williams, Jane (movie character), 39–41, 48, 49
wiseness
  civil rights movement, 87
  and college students, 64–66
  defined, 63–64
  and elementary school students, 60–63
  essay feedback experiment, 64–66, 73, 76–77
  inclusion, wise model of, 128
  leadership by the more empowered, 76–78, 83
  and middle school students, 67–70
  origin of term, 55
  in parent-teacher conferences, 58–59
  risks for the less empowered, 77, 81
  seeing humanity in human differences, 55, 57, 58, 63–64, 71, 75–76, 173–74
  seeing potential in difference, 60, 62–63, 71, 76, 150, 178
  in spite of stereotypes, 58–59
  and trust-building, 58–60, 64, 71, 75–77
  tutors wisely overlooking reputation, 60–63, 150
Won't Lose This Dream (Gumbel), 113, 157
work settings. *See* school and work settings; settings of society

Xavier University in New Orleans, 120

Yale, Elihu, painting of, 92
Yáñez, Marissa Elena, 124–25
Yeager, David, 146

ABOUT THE AUTHOR

Claude M. Steele is currently the Lucie Sterns Professor Emeritus in the Social Sciences at Stanford University (on active duty). He is the author of numerous academic and public-facing articles and the best-selling book *Whistling Vivaldi*, an account of his groundbreaking research on the phenomenon of stereotype threat. He has served in multiple academic leadership roles including the Directorship of the Center for Advanced Study in the Behavioral Sciences, the Dean of Stanford's Graduate School of Education and as provost of both Columbia University and the University of California, Berkeley. He is an elected member of the National Academy of Sciences, the American Academy of Arts and Sciences, and the American Philosophical Society. He has served on the boards of the John D. and Catherine T. MacArthur Foundation, the Russell Sage Foundation, the American Academy of Political Social Sciences, and San Francisco Jazz and is the recipient of honorary doctorates from Yale University, Princeton University, and the University of Chicago, among other universities. He lives in San Francisco, California.